RELATIONSHIP
MILLIONAIRES

TRANSFORM YOUR LOVE INTO YOUR GREATEST ASSET

AN EXCITING CHALLENGE INTO BUILDING
EMOTIONAL WEALTH IN YOUR RELATIONSHIP

D.K. MOENCH

ISBN: 978-1-969463-68-6

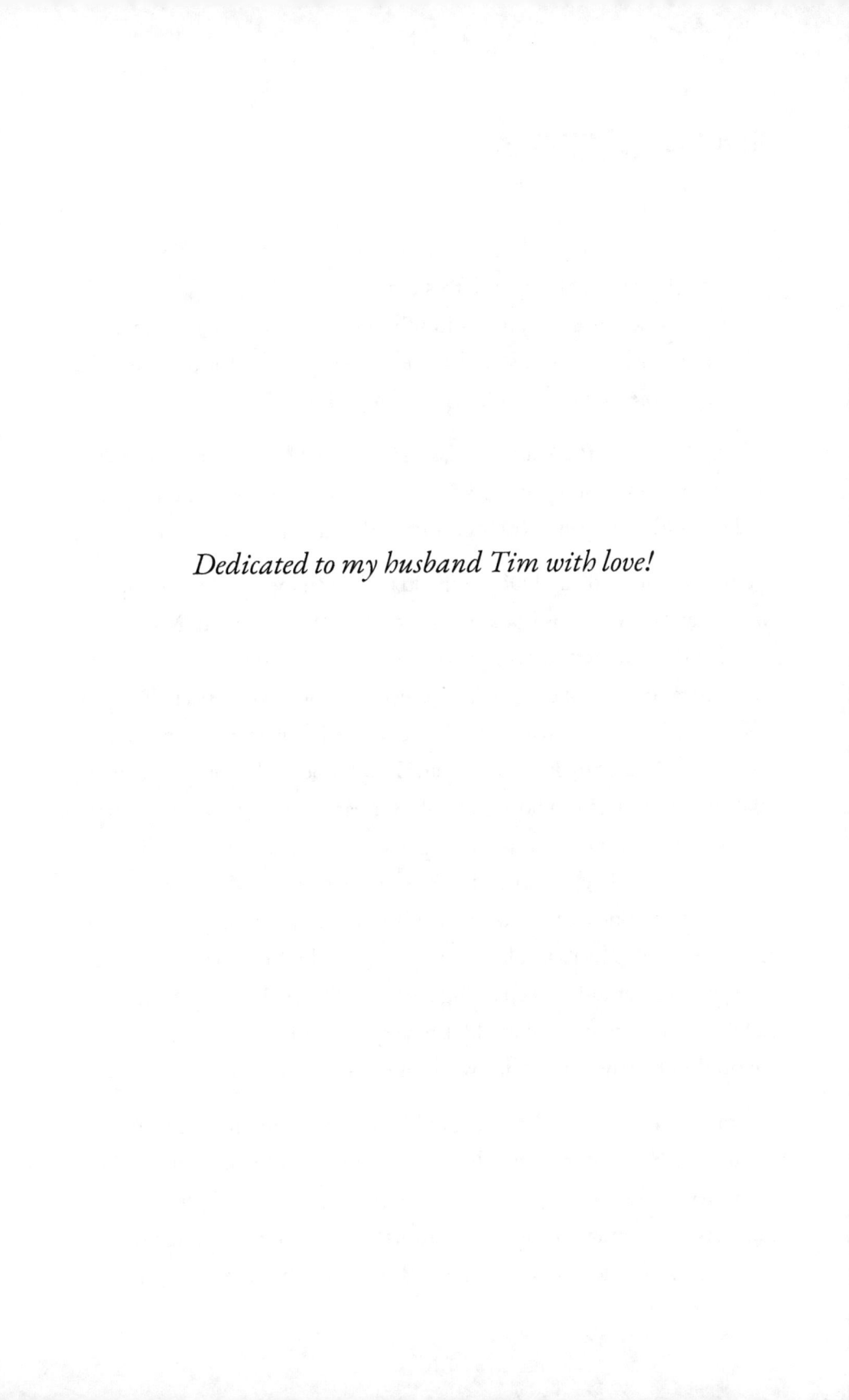

Dedicated to my husband Tim with love!

Acknowledgments

First and foremost, I'd like to thank my husband, Tim. You are my favorite person in the world to be around, and my inspiration for wanting to become a relationship millionaire. Journeying through life with you is my greatest joy, and I'm endlessly grateful for the fun, love, and incredible memories we've created together.

To my Nana and Pa: Your long-lasting marriage has been an inspiration for me. The life you built together is a testament to love, commitment, and joy, and I am so grateful for the countless memories you've given me.

To my parents, Don and Diane: If you had given me a perfect example of what marriage was, this book might not have been written. My parents decided they wanted to do a version of life that made each of them the happiest, and they got divorced. To everyone who has ever been divorced, it's a hard decision to make: the choice to live life apart from the partner that you vowed until death do us part. Death doesn't have to be the thing that parts two people who aren't right for each other. It takes courage to end a relationship that isn't working. I am glad my parents got divorced because they are happier apart than they were together. My mom is a huge supporter of mine and wants wholeheartedly for all my dreams to come true. My dad led by example when something doesn't work out the first time, don't be afraid to keep trying over and over again. My parents both help shape my view of the world. I'm very grateful to them both because I wouldn't be who I am today without them.

To my in-laws, Jim and MaryEllen: They have shown an example of what showing up for each other means when you make a choice you want to last forever. My in-laws have been an example of what partnership is, and in their relationship, they are an outstanding example of bringing out the best in each other. I'm so grateful that they raised my husband. As parents, you don't know what your parenting is going to result in when it comes to your adult children because you don't see the outcome until years later. My husband is the result of my in-laws' combination of two people who made the person in life that I proudly get to call my husband. It was thousands of little things they each did day-to-day that built the man that my husband is today.

To my four sons, Jason, Charlie, Jack, and my fourth baby boy Tommy I'm pregnant with as I write this book: I hope you understand the magnitude that the decision of who you choose to share your life with will be the single greatest decision you ever make. Choosing a partner to journey through life with is so important to the path your life will take. My wish for each of you is to find someone who brings you inner peace and becomes your favorite person to be with. In my opinion, it's the comfort and joy of knowing that your partner brings out the best in you and you bring out the best in them that makes a relationship worth fighting for. Not every day will be perfect and not every day you will bring out the best in each other, but overall, when you take life as a combination when your partner brings you inner peace, that is something worth fighting for.

I'd like to thank the creators behind ChatGPT for the ability to use the tool to aid me and organize my thoughts. I've spent four years dreaming of writing this book, and using ChatGPT has been an amazing gift for me to organize, research, plan, and deliver this book to you all!

Table of Contents

Introduction

Relationship Millionaires was created and inspired by a deep desire to make love the most valuable asset in our lives. I wanted my relationship to be the best it could be—and in that pursuit, I discovered that countless couples share the same struggles, questions, and dreams.

Many of us fall into similar patterns and love gets lost in translation. The problem isn't the lack of love—it's the lack of communication.

I wrote Relationship Millionaires to help couples see each other again—to understand where their partner really is emotionally, mentally, and spiritually. Because when we can see each other clearly, we can build the kind of connection that both can be confident will last a lifetime.

The world today is filled with distractions, pressures, and stressors that pull relationships apart. We're busier, more digitally connected, and emotionally disconnected than ever before. But if not now, when? If love truly is your most important asset, this is the time to invest in it.

This book challenges couples to rebuild communication, restore intimacy, and redefine what success means together. It's for the partners who want to grow, the ones who refuse to give up, and the dreamers who believe that real wealth starts with connection.

I'm not writing this from a pedestal—I'm writing from experience. I married my high school sweetheart, and like many couples, we faced struggles that tested our bond. But through those challenges, I learned the truth that changed everything: when you master connection, you become a relationship millionaire.

The Relationship Millionaires movement is about creating a world where couples lead with love, communicate with honesty, and build with purpose. It's not just a book—it's a challenge, a mirror, and an invitation to make your love deeper.

Together, we'll uncover the habits, emotions, and communication patterns that can transform your relationship from struggling to thriving.

You'll be guided to see your partner differently, speak with empathy, and commit to growth—because love isn't just something you feel, it's something you build.

When you finish this book, I challenge you to take what you've learned, apply it daily, and then pass it along to someone who needs it. That's how we grow stronger—as couples and as a community.

Join the movement, share your journey, and connect with others who are ready to become Relationship Millionaires.

With Love,
D.K. Moench
Relationship Millionaires
Instagram: @relationship.millionaires

CHAPTER 1

Your Future Relationship

"Embrace what you don't know, especially in the beginning, because what you don't know can become your greatest asset." — **Sara Blakely**

The beauty of the future is that it is yet to be seen. Your relationship one year from now does not have to look like it looks today. A good relationship can become great, a great relationship can become extraordinary, and a bad relationship could take a turn and become amazing, or it could get worse. All relationships have the possibility to be anything in the future. It could be good, it could be great, it could be extraordinary, and it also could be worse than it is right now. My hope for you when you read this book and do this challenge is that you take an intentional approach to the most meaningful relationship in your life. My wish is that your relationship improves and you feel more secure in your relationship because you aren't guessing if your spouse is holding their feelings inside. This challenge is all about a flow of open communication so that your relationship can have a knowing of both sides of your inner thoughts. Letting it all out takes vulnerability and trust, and I want to thank you for reading this book and allowing me into your lives.

In the hustle and bustle of daily life, it's easy for couples to drift into routines that feel safe but uninspired. Love, once vibrant and magnetic, can quietly settle into the background as careers, parenting, and responsibilities take center stage. Love, like any other great investment, requires both attention and intention.

We don't just fall into lasting love—we cultivate it. And just as the wealthiest investors strategize for long-term success, if we approach our relationships with a similar level of care and vision, then we have a much greater likelihood of personal fulfillment in our relationships. It's important to understand and become self-aware of what a fulfilling relationship looks like to you and your partner. This book is all about transforming your relationship into your most valuable asset.

When my husband and I first started dating, the connection was undeniable. It didn't take much to feel the spark—late-night conversations, shared dreams, and the effortless feeling of being seen. We were quickly each other's favorite people, and we enjoyed spending as many hours as we could together. But as years passed, life layered on its complexities. There were sleepless nights, financial stress, and moments when we wondered if we would be happier apart. Luckily, we never wondered that for too long. Our wedding highlight video is to the song "Better Together" by Jack Johnson, and for us, we both have continued to feel that even though life can throw a lot at us, we are always better together. That doesn't change the fact that we disagreed a lot and in a lot of different categories. In many moments, we wanted our relationship to get back to the feeling we had when we first got together. I came up with this challenge to see if it would be helpful to us to have better communication.

Through trial and error, we went through life like most married couples. We fought, and then we made up; we tried compromising, and we fought some more. I read book after book that gave advice, and with each piece of expert guidance, I thought, *Why didn't we learn this earlier?* We have now been together over 20 years as I write this book. In the beginning, things were effortless. Then, when they got hard, I quickly realized we didn't have very many tools for handling conflict. In fact, the tools that I was reading about in the relationship books were almost all foreign to me.

I often wondered about what would have happened if we had had these tools before we started arguing. The initial spark of a relationship is enough to last a long while. Years and years after that first spark can fuel a relationship. Reigniting a spark, however, I found to be a challenge. A reignited spark isn't something you hope for—it's something you create. And creating it isn't just about grand romantic gestures. It's about the intentional, everyday actions that build trust, foster joy, and fuel intimacy.

For the entirety of our early relationship, we both described it as great. Then, when things got hard, we struggled at times to find connection. Our foundation was strong, and we could put aside what we were arguing about and enjoy life often, but there were more frequent arguments and frustrations.

There came a time in my marriage when I felt deeply uncertain about how my partner truly saw our relationship. I found myself longing for more clarity, not just during the big conversations, but in the small, everyday moments that shape a marriage. I wanted to feel confident that we were on the same page emotionally, and I needed a way to track our progress as a couple beyond just guessing or hoping things were okay.

I started wondering—how often is it okay to ask, "How are we doing?" without it feeling heavy or exhausting? How do couples stay connected and aligned without always needing a serious sit-down? I imagined what it would be like to replace emotional guesswork with a shared language— something simple, fun, and meaningful that could help partners recognize when things were working... or when they needed a reset.

This book was born from that longing. It's my best attempt to transform uncertainty into a playful, intentional challenge. A way to build connection with curiosity, check-ins with heart, and relationship growth with consistency. Instead of endless days of not knowing, I wanted to create a path where couples could feel seen, supported, and in sync together.

Here's the truth most couples don't talk about: Love alone usually isn't enough. Natural passion wears off, and connection falters without communication. The couples who thrive, who build love that lasts decades, have mastered something essential. They treat their relationship like a growing, evolving, ever-changing, and precious piece of their life.

This book is your invitation to do the same. We're going to treat love like the ultimate investment—a challenge to build emotional, spiritual, and lifelong connection. Because the health of your partnership doesn't just impact your relationship; it influences your family, your work, and your legacy. Whether you are starting this challenge with negative or positive thoughts about your relationship, the end goal is the same for everyone. A secure and loving relationship where both parties to the relationship feel that the overall relationship is amazing! The mark of the goal to get there: one million relationship dollars!

What is a relationship dollar? It's a form of keeping track of your relationship in the form of a fictitious money account. There are plenty of actual millionaires who have miserable marriages, and plenty of people with very little money in the bank who have phenomenal relationships. For most people, I don't see a strict correlation between monetary wealth and a good relationship. If I had to pick between being a relationship millionaire and a monetary millionaire, I would pick a relationship millionaire every single time. Ideally, I would like to be both an actual millionaire and a relationship millionaire. However, if I had to pick only one, it would be a relationship millionaire with very little money in my bank account versus having a million dollars in the bank and a poor relationship.

So, what does it take to be a relationship millionaire? A relationship millionaire in the context of this book is a challenge to start with $0 and work your way to $1,000,000 relationship dollars by adding things your partner does to fill your love tank and subtracting when your partner does something to drain your love tank. When you get to $1,000,000 as a team, you are officially relationship millionaires according to this challenge. If you are already feeling like relationship millionaires, you can challenge yourself to see how quickly you can get to a million. If you are currently feeling as though your relationship is running on fumes and in the negative relationship dollars, then this is the perfect challenge for you to take a chance that this will be the tool that helps you to make changes in your relationship.

You might be wondering, "Why a challenge to a million?" Challenges push us outside our comfort zones. They ignite creativity and require us to show up for our partner and our relationship. Just as fitness challenges transform bodies and financial challenges grow bank accounts, this relationship challenge is designed to help you and your partner rediscover your potential together.

Over the next chapters, we'll dive into the rules of the challenge and expert insights to help you tackle this challenge head-on. Whether your relationship is thriving or in need of repair, this is your chance to shift gears, reframe your connection, and set a course for a brighter future.

So, what does it take to become "relationship millionaires"? Let's start with the basics. Wealth in love isn't measured in the same way as money is. Love is personal, and what fills one person's love tank doesn't equally fill another person's. You and your partner don't share the same desires, and your love tank is likely filled and drained in very different ways. Love can have resilience during hard times, and a strong foundation can get you through a lot of rough patches. The moments you choose each other, even when it's hard, show a lasting relationship. When a love tank is drained so far that you are running on empty, drastic measures can save a relationship, but continuing down the path of an empty love tank is hard on everyone involved. If you are struggling, think about a car that has run out of gas: You could push it everywhere you go as a new method of getting your family places, but that is hard. Instead, you could push your vehicle with the aim of getting to a gas station to refuel. That plan makes a lot more sense. It's okay to push your car temporarily to get to a gas station. It's not a good idea to change the way you use your car to put it in neutral and push it everywhere. Some relationships have one or both parties feeling like they are stuck in neutral, and they can't find a gas station to refuel. Or they have found a gas station, but their gas tank has a crack in it, and refilling it quickly drains it because of the leak. In the case of a gas tank that has a crack in it, you may benefit from a combination of a relationship therapist and this book. Only you know the specifics of your relationship. I hope to provide you with resources to improve from where you are today, no matter where you start.

My hope for you and your relationship is that you build a healthy perspective on a love tank. It's natural for it to be filled and drained. It's not a one-way, only filling, never draining. It is completely natural for a love tank to be drained and refilled in an endless cycle. The issue comes in relationships when a love tank gets drained without getting refilled, and you are operating on fumes, grasping at the little bits of love tank additions that are far outweighed by draining.

There is a difference between a gas tank in a car naturally using gas to get from one place to another, draining, and then going to the gas station to refuel, and a gas tank that has been in a car accident and needs to go to the body shop to be replaced. Either way, you can do this! You can be intentional about becoming relationship millionaires. You just might need a fresh restart, which is what this challenge does for you.

That doesn't mean you don't bring up the past! Quite the opposite. When past actions hurt you, it drains your love tank, and that's okay; you should bring it up. But the important part is to drain in a healthy way, where you are bringing up the past to heal and not to have an open wound. Drain and refill, drain and refill, on repeat. Things that have hurt you will drain your tank faster, kind of like going uphill will naturally burn more fuel. When the past resurfaces, it's important to let your partner know in some way: "This is a metaphorical hill for me, and when you do that, my love tank gets drained faster than driving on flat ground." It's also important that you don't look at your car and think, "We should just keep it parked in the driveway so it doesn't use any gas. If we never move it, the gas tank will stay full." That is like never sharing your conflicting feelings, and not telling your partner that something they did upset you. Long-term, it's not a healthy way to live. Learning the natural flow of filling up and draining in a healthy way, where draining doesn't feel threatening, instead, it feels natural, is ideal.

Think of your relationship as a garden. Without regular care, even the most beautiful garden can become overrun with weeds or fall into neglect. But with attention—watering the soil, pruning the plants, and planting fresh seeds—it can flourish.

The same goes for your love life. Neglect leads to distance, but small, consistent actions—a surprise date night, a handwritten note, or a shared moment of laughter—can reignite the spark. Once your spark is reignited, you are on your way to becoming relationship millionaires. This challenge will give you the tools to nurture your "garden" and help it bloom like never before. Once you have established a relationship millionaire status, the challenge is complete. This isn't something to do and keep track of forever. Think of it more like redoing your garden entirely and getting all fresh landscaping. Once you are complete, you give it some water and pull the occasional weed, but the work of the entire transformation is already done.

Throughout this journey, I'll share stories of couples who transform their relationships by embracing this challenge. Any stories based on real couples will have their names changed to respect their privacy. Some start on shaky ground, barely able to communicate. Others were happy but craved deeper intimacy. Regardless of where they began, they all found one common truth: building wealth in love is a decision, not a destination.

You'll also find expert advice from relationship therapists like my personal favorite, Dr. John Gottman, and practical exercises to strengthen your bond. These aren't cookie-cutter solutions—they're tailored to help you and your partner uncover what works best for you.

Building wealth in love requires a shared vision. Just as business partners align on goals, values, and strategies, successful couples do the same. They dream together. They problem-solve together. They build a foundation of mutual respect, and most importantly, they celebrate wins—big and small—along the way.

But before we dive into the challenge itself, let's pause to reflect. What brought you to this book?

Partner A

_____

_____

Partner B

_____

_____

Maybe you're looking for inspiration, or maybe you've hit a roadblock in your relationship. Whatever the reason, know this: The fact that you're here, willing to do the work, is already a sign of success. Be grateful that your partner is willing to take on this challenge. There are plenty of couples where one partner sees a metaphorical garden overtaken with weeds, and has a partner who doesn't want to take part in improving their situation. This book is not only for couples who have a negative relationship. Some couples have a great relationship, and they want to make it even better. In either case, this is a challenge that will take a minimum of 40 days. The rules of the challenge will be laid out in the chapters as you journey through the book.

Let's break down the mindset to get into before you begin. The relationship millionaire mindset is one to adopt, understanding that the status of relationship millionaire is entirely within your control because you are the ones who are in charge of adding and subtracting money. Running a marathon isn't going 25 miles and saying, "Good job, let's stop now." A marathon is a full 26.2 miles. Running 25 miles is great exercise, but it isn't a full marathon. The million-dollar goal is important to reach in order to declare yourselves relationship millionaires. As we embark on this journey, I want you to embrace one simple truth: love is a practice. It's not something that just happens; it's something we do. And like any practice, it takes effort, patience, and a willingness to learn.

This book isn't about perfection—it's about progress. It's about showing up for your partner, even when it's hard. It's about giving grace, asking for what you need, and finding joy in the process of growing together.

Are you ready to begin? The first step is to commit. Commit to yourself, to your partner, and to the challenge. Over the next pages, we'll break down the rules and then give suggestions on tools, strategies, and mindsets that will help you succeed.

CHAPTER 2

Encouragement to Be Open to Trying the Relationship Millionaires Challenge

"If you want something you've never had, you must be willing to do something you've never done."
— **Thomas Jefferson**

Embarking on something new can feel intimidating, especially when it comes to your relationship. The familiar is comfortable, even when it's not ideal. But growth happens when we step outside of our comfort zones and embrace the unknown. That's exactly what the *Relationship Millionaires Challenge* invites you to do—step into uncharted territory with your partner and discover just how much closer, stronger, and more connected you can become.

Why This Challenge Matters

Think of your relationship as a garden, as described in the previous chapter. Without regular care, even the most beautiful garden can become overrun with weeds or fall into neglect. The *Relationship Millionaires Challenge* is like a revitalization project for your love—it's a chance to water the soil, plant new seeds, and remove the metaphorical weeds that are the habits or behaviors that no longer serve you.

By tracking small, everyday moments with the Relationship Cash Register, you'll become more intentional about how you give and receive love. You'll also gain clarity about the things that strengthen your connection and the actions that unintentionally cause distance.

Breaking Free from Routine

One of the biggest hurdles in any long-term relationship is routine. Routines can be helpful, but they can also lull us into complacency. The challenge is designed to shake things up and bring a fresh perspective to your partnership.

Imagine this: Instead of ending your day feeling disconnected, you and your partner reflect on your actions, share moments of appreciation, and even have a little fun deciding how much "relationship currency" you earned that day. It's not just about tracking progress—it's about deepening your awareness and fostering joy in the process.

The Power of Commitment

Committing to this challenge isn't about perfection—it's about showing up. It's about saying, "I choose us, even on the hard days." By taking on this challenge, you're making a declaration: Your relationship is worth the effort.

It's natural to feel some hesitation. What if it doesn't work? What if my partner doesn't fully engage? These thoughts are valid, but they're also opportunities for growth. Remember, the act of trying is, in itself, an act of love. Every small step you take together strengthens the foundation of your relationship.

Letting Go of Fear

Trying something new requires vulnerability. It asks you to let go of the fear of failure and embrace the possibility of transformation.

The *Relationship Millionaires Challenge* isn't about creating a perfect relationship—it's about creating an honest, intentional, and fulfilling one.

This process will ask you to have conversations you might have been avoiding. It will encourage you to look at your habits and reflect on the ways you can grow, both individually and as a couple. Most importantly, it will invite you to have fun together—to laugh, celebrate, and rediscover the reasons you fell in love in the first place.

You may not both have the same idea of what a weed is and what needs to be pulled. Dandelions are some of the cutest, sweetest things that my sons pull for me and give me a bouquet of. I love it when my kiddos pick a bouquet of dandelions! But technically, dandelions are weeds. When my husband mows the lawn, he shortens the grass, but he also gets rid of all the dandelions that my sons love to pick and I love to receive. Two things can be true at the same time. You can be sad that the dandelions go away when the lawn gets mowed, and you can also appreciate the effort your partner put into mowing the lawn. There are times when it may feel like bringing up the fact that you are sad when the dandelion weeds go away makes your partner think internally, *Does her being sad that I'm cutting 'weeds' mean she doesn't want me to mow the lawn anymore?* Or they might think it's impossible to please you. *How could I possibly keep the dandelion weeds to keep you and our kids happy, and at the same time shorten the grass?* That request seems like "I can't please you, and it's impossible to accomplish." One partner can feel sad at the loss of weeds and also fully understand that the dandelions being swept up in the lawnmower are the natural course of lawn care. They want you to mow the lawn and also acknowledge that they love a long lawn that gives the opportunity to pull dandelion weeds. That doesn't mean that they don't love it when their kids pick the dandelion weeds. It's all about perspective and hearing your partner's communication.

Action Step

Sit down with your partner and talk about what excites you most about the challenge. Share any concerns you have and set the intention to support each other throughout the journey.

CHAPTER 3

The Story of How the Book Idea Originated

"Every great dream begins with a dreamer."
— **Harriet Tubman**

When I was in elementary school, I had an experience that I now credit as the foundation for this book, even though the idea for the book came to me 25 years later. The seed was planted in me as a child.

In sixth grade, three new students joined our class throughout the year, each from a different country: India, China, and Venezuela. I remember thinking how hard it would be for me to move to another country and try to do dittos in another language. I especially thought, *What if I moved to China and there were pictures instead of words?* How confusing would that be? These students often struggled with assignments involving English-heavy subjects like Science or Social Studies. But when the class was given math assignments—especially those without word problems—they zipped right through, completing the work faster than almost everyone else.

I was fascinated by this. It struck me that numbers are universal; they transcend language barriers in a way that words cannot. I couldn't help but wonder how quickly they would finish assignments in their native languages. This thought stayed with me, quietly shaping how I viewed communication, understanding, and connection.

Fast-forward to my adult life and marriage. My husband and I, like most couples, found ourselves caught in cycles of miscommunication and misunderstanding.

Despite our best efforts, small irritations would spiral into arguments, and I couldn't help but feel frustrated. Then, I discovered *The 5 Love Languages* by Gary Chapman. It was a revelation! Finally, a framework to honor and understand each other's love languages.

But there was a catch: speaking a love language that isn't natural to you is hard. It's not as extreme as learning a new spoken language, but it can feel similarly unnatural. I often found myself trying to explain to my husband that my failure to express love in his preferred love language wasn't a lack of love—it was just that my instincts didn't align with his preferences. We were constantly showing love in our native preferred love languages and wondering why it wasn't being received and reciprocated.

Then, I had a thought: *What if, instead of arguing and trying to find the perfect words, we used numbers?* Numbers are universal. Numbers can be calculated, understood, and quantified.

This was the beginning of what I initially called the *Relationship Cash Register*.

The Birth of a System

The idea was simple: Instead of getting bogged down in disagreements, we could assign a number to things that irritated us, clearly state it, and then move on. If we agreed that we both had times where we knew it was natural to irritate each other, if we assign a number instead of explaining in words, I thought it had the potential to be a better system. No more long-winded arguments, fewer misunderstandings—just a quick acknowledgment. To me, it was a brilliant system with the potential to transform our communication.

There was only one problem:

My husband hated it.

He had plenty of reasons why:

- "It takes too much time."
- "It feels like extra work."
- "I don't want to do it."

At first, I took it personally. My anxious attachment kicked in full force. *How could he not want to do this with me?* I thought. *Does that mean he doesn't care? Doesn't love me?* In my mind, it was such a simple, helpful idea—why resist something that could make our lives easier?

But years later, I stumbled upon a recommendation in a Facebook group run by Jimmy on Relationship—a book called *Secure Love* by Julie Menanno. It cracked something open for me.

In it, Menanno writes:

> "When we feel unsafe in connection, we tend to resort to our attachment coping mechanisms—anxious partners pursue and protest, while avoidant partners withdraw and shut down."

Suddenly, it all made sense. My husband wasn't trying to reject me or sabotage our progress—he was simply protecting himself in the way his nervous system had learned to. He leans towards being avoidant. I lean towards being anxious. And that dynamic, I learned, is actually incredibly common in relationships.

So, when he said, "I don't want to do it," it wasn't about a lack of love. It was about his discomfort. For me, the idea of skipping emotional check-ins felt like neglect. For him, it felt like overwhelm.

We needed a way to speak to each other from the lens of understanding, not blame. That's what *Secure Love* taught me: that love isn't just passion or commitment—it's built on emotional safety.

We tried the system—eventually. He agreed, after about the tenth time I asked. We did it for a week. And while it didn't stick then, it planted a seed. That seed would grow into the idea for this book. What about a challenge where, at the end of it, you really felt like you had secure love! The relationship cash register system had no end, just an idea. The relationship millionaire model had a clear destination and a goal that couples could feel really accomplished once they achieved. Like running a marathon, when you are complete, you feel an extreme sense of accomplishment. So, my idea evolved from the original Relationship Cash Register to the challenge to become Relationship Millionaires.

* * *

Try This Together

1. Which attachment style do you identify with most?

(Anxious, Avoidant, or Secure?)

Write a short reflection here:

You: _____

Your Partner: _____

2. On a scale from 1 to 10, how much do you want to do this challenge?

(1 = Only doing it for my partner, 10 = Fully excited and ready)

    Partner 1: Name _____ Rank _____
    Partner 2: Name _____ Rank _____

Remember:

If your partner is at a 1, it doesn't mean you should take it as a sign that they don't love you—it might simply mean they experience closeness differently. Often, avoidant partners fear being overwhelmed or "not enough," just as anxious partners fear being too much or abandoned.

What matters most is that you're both showing up—even imperfectly.

I wasn't deterred by my husband's lack of wanting to do this challenge, but I was confused. I kept asking, trying to show him how much easier and less emotionally draining this system could make our lives. *Why do I have to ask ten times for you to agree? Why did he shut down and stop participating after a week?* Looking back, it is probably credited to his emotionally avoidant tendencies that he would rather not do something so detail-oriented. For an anxious attachment style, it is a dream to be able to journal and keep track of everything you and your partner do to fill and drain each other's love tanks. Please understand this book is written by someone who has an anxious attachment style! If you are in a relationship with someone who leans towards an avoidant attachment style, you should be so incredibly grateful that they are willing to get out of their comfort zone for you! There is a way to honor that difference.

You can also try to make sure that you and your partner understand the extreme value of making each other feel safe and secure to create secure love.

Since I have a more anxious personality, I asked ChatGPT to write a note to anyone who leans towards avoidant for the purposes of this challenge.

From ChatGPT to You

Your avoidant patterns developed for a reason. Maybe you grew up needing to self-soothe. Maybe it felt safer to rely on yourself than to trust someone who might let you down. That makes sense. Your nervous system adapted beautifully to help you survive—and even succeed—in environments where vulnerability felt risky.

But this challenge isn't your childhood. And your partner isn't the same person who disappointed you in the past. This is a chance to update the story. You can be in a relationship that honors your need for space and your partner's need for connection. They're not opposites—they're complementary when navigated with care.

Even if emotional expression isn't your strength, you can still be a powerful partner. You don't have to dive into deep feelings every day. But saying, "I hear you," or "I'm trying," or "This is new for me, but I care," can change everything.

Secure love doesn't mean you never pull back—it means you always return. Show your partner that you're here, even if it's hard. Not because you're being forced, but because deep down, you want a relationship that's steady, respectful, and real.

And yes, you're worthy of that kind of love.

Attachment Is a Sliding Scale

It's important to know that attachment styles—whether anxious, avoidant, or secure—aren't rigid labels. They exist on a sliding scale, and we can shift along that scale depending on our current stress levels, life circumstances, past experiences, and even how safe we feel in a particular relationship.

Someone who is generally avoidant may feel more secure when they're with a partner who is calm, communicative, and non-judgmental. On the flip side, they may feel more avoidant when they're overwhelmed, triggered, or asked to be vulnerable in a way that feels too fast or unfamiliar.

Likewise, someone with an anxious attachment style may feel much more secure when their partner offers consistency, reassurance, and open communication—but more anxious when they sense distance, withdrawal, or mixed messages.

You're not boxed in. Your attachment style isn't a diagnosis—it's a pattern. And patterns can evolve.

This is why the challenge you're about to do matters. It's not just about who you are today; it's about who you are becoming together.

The goal is not perfection—it's progress.

And progress happens when both partners can recognize their triggers, offer grace, and communicate through discomfort with honesty and care.

From Numbers to a Million-Dollar Goal

During that week, I came up with an idea to make the system more exciting: What if we set a goal to accumulate one million *relationship dollars*? Every act of kindness, understanding, and connection would add to our balance, while moments of irritation or miscommunication would subtract from it.

I added a twist: Once we reached a million, we'd celebrate with a big reward—something fun and meaningful that we could both look forward to.

At first, I was thrilled by the concept. It combined accountability with fun, and it turned the abstract work of building a relationship into something tangible and measurable. But as the week went on, it became clear that my husband still wasn't on board. He found the system tedious, and I realized that my vision needed some refining.

Expanding on the Five Love Languages

Gary Chapman's five love languages—words of affirmation, quality time, acts of service, receiving gifts, and physical touch—offer a revolutionary way to understand how people give and receive love. But translating those languages into everyday life isn't always easy.

Numbers offer a bridge. If one partner thrives on acts of service, cleaning the kitchen might earn $2,000 relationship dollars. While someone who has acts of service low on their list might have cleaning the kitchen at $100. In a relationship, the kitchen still has to get cleaned, and one partner constantly doing all the cleaning might build resentment. Maybe a partner who often doesn't clean the kitchen might be able to express to their partner that when they attempted to clean the kitchen, they were given $200. After not loading the dishwasher correctly and putting things that were not dishwasher-safe inside, and receiving the comment "What are you, a child who hasn't learned to read yet? Can't you see that the bottom of this bowl says hand wash only?" That comment drained the love tank $5,000. So, this person got credit for $200 and drained themselves $5,000. It makes sense why their body would want to protect them from doing the dishes in the future.

I urge you that it's time to create a blank slate around your conflicts. It is so important for this challenge not to ignore your past hurts but to instead communicate how your love tank is drained.

Meanwhile, for a partner who values physical touch, a simple, spontaneous hug might be worth $750. And another person might deduct for a hug. When they forgot to take the garbage out and then tried to give a hug to make up for it, your body felt irritated, and your love tank was drained $200. Does that mean that the partner who was upset about the garbage cans doesn't want to engage in hugs? No, absolutely not. However, when you are rejected from a hug, it's hard for the brain to distinguish and compartmentalize why the rejection happened. This challenge can help alleviate that. If you are specific in your communication, you can use a number to make things clearer. "I deducted $200 in this instance because your parents are coming to visit next week, and I don't want garbage overflowing when we are having company."

Then, the other partner might say, "I've been working late to finish the landscaping so that when our company comes over, we have a nice front garden bed, and because of that, it might be why I forgot to take out the trash. Also, my love tank is drained because ever since the beginning of our relationship, it has been solely my job to take out the trash. I don't mind doing it, but when I forget, you get mad at me when I've taken the garbage out hundreds of times, and I don't hear a thank you for any of the times I have done it, and you don't do it ever."

The important thing here is to quantify your love tank and explain it. Taking the garbage out can give $100, and not taking the garbage out can deduct $5,000. That is okay because that is how you might feel in the moment. Does it make sense that a person has to take the garbage out 50 times in a year to make up for the $5,000 loss to the love tank? No, that is why we show love, receive love, and give love in very different ways!

As Chapman writes, "Love is something you do for someone else, not something you do for yourself." By using the relationship cash register, couples can step outside their own preferences and focus on what truly matters to their partner.

Love Languages and Journaling

Understanding love languages is a good step in building emotional wealth. Take a moment to reflect on how you and your partner express and receive love. Use the space below to rank the five love languages in order of importance for each of you.

Partner A: My Love Languages
(1 = most important, 5 = least important)

1.

2.

3.

4.

5.

Partner B: My Love Languages
(1 = most important, 5 = least important)

1.

2.

3.

4.

5.

The Evolution of the Idea

Even though the *Relationship Cash Register* didn't stick with us at that time, the idea stayed with me. I began to wonder: *What if this system could help other couples? What if it could be adapted into a challenge that wasn't just about resolving conflict but also about fostering joy, connection, and intentionality?*

That's when I started envisioning the *Relationship Millionaires Challenge* as a tool for couples to build emotional wealth. It's not just about resolving differences; it's about celebrating the relationship you're building and treating it as your greatest investment.

CHAPTER 4

Setting a Reward for the End of the Challenge

"Setting goals is the first step in turning the invisible into the visible." — **Tony Robbins**

You've committed to something extraordinary—a challenge that asks more of your relationship than the day-to-day ever has. And because of that, your reward shouldn't be ordinary either.

This chapter is your invitation to dream together. To sit down, look each other in the eye, and ask:

What would feel like the ultimate celebration of us?

Something that says:

We've built something real. We're Relationship Millionaires.

This reward should be something you both want. Something that lights you up, not just as individuals, but as a team. A vision that requires you both to be excited about the outcome!

Think big. Think bold.

- Is it a trip you've been dreaming of?
- A vow renewal ceremony with your kids there to witness?
- A shared investment in something you believe in—a home, a legacy, a mission?

Whatever it is, make it worthy of your work together. This challenge won't always be easy. But your reward? That's the fuel to keep you moving forward—together.

While this should be a big reward, it should also match your financial means. Don't set a reward that is going to stress someone out, so that they feel uncomfortable that you will have the financial resources to make it happen. Be very careful to find that Goldilocks reward that feels just right. Not too big, not too small, something that is going to be really exciting for you both, but not a financial burden.

There's no one forcing you to do this. You decided to do this challenge because you want more from your relationship. And the truth is, what you're building can't be bought—but it can be celebrated.

Let the reward be something that reminds you:

We did this. We did it together. And it was worth it!

Once you come up with your reward, write it down here.

_____

_____

_____

_____

Now, the next step is to write three letters to each other for checkpoints along the way.

These letters will become vision anchors—a way for you to connect emotionally with your future selves before the journey begins.

Letter 1: When you reach $100,000

You have committed to this process long enough to get to $100,000, and you are doing well. The day you pass $100,000, you get to open your first letter.

Theme of the Letter: Encouragement & confidence to continue.

Include in your letter: What strengths do you see in your partner? What strength do you see in your relationship?

Letter 2: When you reach $500,000

Theme of the letter: Confidence to get to the finish line.

This is your halfway checkpoint. Life gets busy, and let's be honest, writing down and keeping track of your fictitious love tank relationship dollars throughout this journey isn't always going to be your top priority. We all live in the real world with real money, real stresses, and real obligations. This letter should be encouragement to keep going through the second half of the challenge and become relationship millionaires. $500,000 puts you in a pretty secure place. You are doing great. At this point, you should feel confident that you have a solid relationship. Don't run 13 miles in a marathon and say, "Let's get lunch, we did a solid exercise today." You signed up for the challenge, and the goal is ONE MILLION RELATIONSHIP DOLLARS!!!

Let's get to the finish line. Tell your partner all the wonderful things you love about them in this letter and why it's important to you to get to the reward.

Letter 3: When you reach the ultimate $1,000,000

Theme: We did it!

The moment you cross the threshold into becoming relationship millionaires, you get to take a snapshot in time back to where you started. I hope that at the point where you finish the challenge, you both feel a real sense of accomplishment! Like a marathon, you chose to do this challenge. You can go right on living the way you are living in your relationship without ever starting this challenge. But if you do decide to start and you do decide to finish, I am confident you will feel a sense of closeness and connection with each other, and that you have a solid relationship. You have accomplished a goal you set together, and now it's time for your reward.

Take your time and write as much as possible. Then seal your letters and put them in a meaningful place so they are not opened until the checkpoints and the challenge are complete!

If one of you likes to write long letters and the other partner writes short letters, that's okay! It is unlikely that you will both have the same writing style, and you can honor that difference. For partners who aren't excited about writing down their letters, try not to stress about writing these three letters. If writing down these letters is outside your comfort zone, get started acknowledging it can be the first step to a closer relationship with your partner.

As I mentioned earlier, one partner might be more excited about this challenge each step of the way, while the other partner could be more avoidant of certain situations. That is so common, and try your best not to think that if your partner doesn't want to do this challenge, that means they don't care about the relationship. Our comfort zones are different, and our life experiences are different. The willingness to do this challenge is not a direct reflection of how much your partner cares about you. If writing a letter is difficult for one partner, it does not mean they don't care; it could mean a variety of other things. They may have been told by a teacher at some point that they aren't a good writer, they might suffer from undiagnosed dyslexia, they might have written a letter in the past where they poured their heart out and were broken up with immediately after, and they are worried about writing another letter to you. There are countless reasons why someone might not want to write a letter, but at the same time be fully invested in the relationship and a worthy partner. It's important to keep your own inner negative self-talk to a minimum and give your partner every single benefit of the doubt that your relationship can be extraordinary!

If your partner is currently avoidant, it doesn't mean they can't change to make your relationship work. It more than likely means they have something inside them that is making them uncomfortable. This challenge is an attempt to make both parties to the relationship feel seen and heard, and make progress along the way numerically, which is much more universally understood. My hope is that the numbers can bridge the gaps in communication styles so that you can make meaningful changes in your relationship to make both parties feel a more secure love.

Try your best with these three letters because you have a chance to preserve a snapshot in time and write a letter to your future self and future partner. Remember, your future self and future partner do not have to be anything like who you are today. Keep all the good parts and try your best to leave the less-than-desirable parts of you in the past. These letters are a great way to visualize your future self and acknowledge that, as humans, we can change our behaviors, change our habits, and improve the closeness of our relationships.

Once you are finished signing the letters, put them in an envelope, and sign the flap of the envelope. Please, please, please do not prematurely open the letters! I know it can be tempting to read what your partner wrote about you, but it's an important part of the process to have delayed gratification on first getting to the goal and then opening the letters.

CHAPTER 5

The Rules of the Challenge

"Small disciplines repeated with consistency every day lead to great achievements gained slowly over time."
— **John Maxwell**

Finally!

This challenge isn't about keeping score—it's about becoming aware. It's about building wealth in the emotional bank account of your relationship. When your emotional bank account is overflowing and you have a setback, you can better gauge where you are in your overall relationship.

Why is a marathon 26.2 miles? In 1908, the Olympics were held in London, and organizers planned the marathon to start at Windsor Castle and finish in front of the Royal Box at the Olympic Stadium, so that the royal family could watch the finish.

- The distance from Windsor Castle to the stadium was 26 miles.
- But to place the finish line exactly in front of the royal viewing box, an extra 385 yards (0.2 miles) was added.

The Result

That made the race 26.2 miles, and in 1921, the International Amateur Athletic Federation (now World Athletics) officially adopted this distance as the standard for all marathons.

I'm creating a standard of rules in the effort to help couples communicate better and improve their relationships!

My heart is truly in a place of wanting to help people and add to society, becoming a more beautiful and harmonic place to have more peace in our everyday lives.

The rules aren't here to restrict you. They're here to guide you toward each other, especially when life challenges seem to be pulling you apart. It's possible that with some couples, these rules could make their relationship a bit more rocky before it becomes transformative. That is to be expected for some. If you are both growth-oriented people, then you will likely have less struggle. If one of you likes things to remain the same and comfortable, then naturally introducing a daily assignment for them when they previously didn't have to do this at all is likely going to be a point of frustration.

I want to congratulate you on making it this far in the book to get to the rules. The rules I've laid out here are a framework. I hope that you can adopt them and try them the same way a city that hosts a marathon sets it up to be 26.2 miles. I tried to make the rules as simple as possible.

Rule 1: You award and subtract money from the relationship cash register based on your love tank draining and filling.

For any one single event, you can not award or subtract more than $5,000. If something feels like more than $5,000, you can let your partner know, but for the purposes of the challenge, the single event cap is $5,000 for one thing per day. That does not mean $5,000 in total over the challenge for a certain behavior; it means $5,000 cap for one single entry per day.

You are recording both interactions and emotions. The same exact event that occurs one day may drain your love tank $400, and another day, the exact same interaction may drain you $2,000; that's okay to bring awareness to that. Your emotional state matters and is important to the honesty and integrity of the challenge.

Rule 2: At the end of the day, you combine both partners' daily amounts to get a sum total for the day.

For every day, there is a daily cap of $25,000 in either positive or negative direction. If it's less than $25,000, use the amount that is the sum total. You are in this together, and both of you have a daily amount that represents your day that you combine at the end of the day. I encourage you, if you have the energy at the end of the day, if you as a couple seem like you will be ending in the negative, try to ask your partner for ways that you can bring your collective contribution up.

Example 1:
Partner A total +$17,500
Partner B total −$6,200

The result is that the couple's daily total towards the million for this day is +$11,300. You would add this amount to your total and move $11,300 towards your million-dollar goal.

Example 2:
Partner A total −$21,000
Partner B total +$5,500

The result is that the couple's daily total towards the million for this day is −$15,500.

You would subtract this amount from your total and move $15,500 away from the million-dollar goal.

Example 3:
Partner A total +$44,000
Partner B total +$7,000

The result is that the couple's daily total towards the million for this day is +$51,000. You would apply the cap rule and only add $25,000. Don't be afraid to go over the cap and know that you did amazingly that day! For the purposes of the challenge, the reason for the cap is that this challenge takes a minimum of 40 days to complete if you hit the $25,000 cap each day. This gives you time to participate in the challenge instead of having a few hundred thousand dollars days and saying we are done with the challenge in less than a week. The period of 40 days is a good amount of time to really immerse yourself in the challenge.

Rule 3: Switch roles on the 1st and 15th of the month

On the 1st and 15th of every month, instead of giving your partner money for the things they do, you'll give yourself money for everything you do, and you won't be evaluating your partner at all on these days.

Take inventory of what you've done for the household, kids, business, or relationship. This is not about ego—it's about awareness. The awareness goes both for yourself and your partner. It's very important for you to be very detailed during these days.

These days are for honest self-reflection. It's a way to see your relationship not just through your own eyes, but through the eyes of your partner.

The switching roles challenge days are supposed to be used as a mirror to reflect on yourself and how you see yourself showing up in your marriage.

On the 1st and 15th of every month, each partner becomes their own bookkeeper. Instead of assigning value to your partner's actions, you turn the spotlight inward on yourself. Now is your chance to showcase all that you do for your partner!

This is your chance to ask:

- How am I showing up in this relationship?
- What do I do behind the scenes that deserves appreciation, even from myself?
- What might I be doing (or not doing) that is draining my partner's love tank?

This is not a time to seek external validation—it's a time to grow in self-awareness.

How it works:

Each partner calculates how much money they would "earn" for their efforts—chores, communication, kindness, emotional labor, problem-solving, and work stress handled.

This is not about justifying your value to your partner—this is about bringing visibility and appreciation to your unseen efforts.

At the same time, you are encouraged to subtract money from your own total for moments when you knowingly added tension, avoided connection, broke a promise, or caused emotional harm—however minor or unintentional.

It's not just about what you do. It's how you do it.

If one partner goes to a demanding job, don't just say "$500 for work." Detail your inner world:

- "I held it together when a shipment was delayed, and I wanted to explode."
- "I pushed through three rejections in a row to make that last sale, because I want to support our future."

These moments matter. They are often invisible when your partner isn't with you when they happen. The moments are emotional labor—and they deserve recognition.

Emotional Honesty: The Key to Growth

This rule is not about punishment or perfection—it's about truth and self-growth and the ability to share your world with your partner when they aren't around. Coming home from a stressful day at work doesn't have to feel like you are bottling everything up inside. You may be surprised that your partner can support you and make you feel better after a tough day at work.

If you came home late without communicating, and you know your partner has a deep trigger around lateness because of childhood trauma, acknowledge that. Don't just say "Oops." Subtract money. Why? Because it costs your partner emotionally—even if you didn't mean to.

Each partner's triggers will assign different weights to different actions. What feels like a minor infraction to one partner may feel like abandonment to the other.

That's the power of this rule: It opens the door to quantifying the emotional landscape of your relationship.

A New Way to Be Seen

When you switch roles, you're not just doing this for you—you're letting your partner into your inner world. This exercise creates empathy and trust. It shows your partner that you're paying attention to your own behavior and that you're courageous enough to admit when you fall short.

Don't skimp on these days. Go deep. Be detailed. Take this time to pat yourself on the back for all you do to show up in your relationship!

It can be hard for some people to take this opportunity to really bring the spotlight on themselves. These days might be really challenging for some of the partners participating in the challenge. It might take a few times for the 1st and 15th of the month to come and go, and for you to really get into the groove of showing off all you're for your relationship, that's okay! Try not to bottle things up inside, and give yourself money on the 15th for things you have done the week prior. While your efforts deserve to be celebrated, this challenge really is about how you are showing up on the specific day, so try your best to keep your monetary additions and subtractions to only events that have happened on the day you are currently living.

Honor Your Partner and Their Experience

A word of caution: You might have a reaction to having money deducted and wish your partner would share less and bottle up more inside. That approach could lead to long-term resentment. There is a balance between sharing every single thought you have and not sharing enough with your partner to be emotionally vulnerable. Some couples, when they do this, have an imbalance of entries. One partner carefully details dozens of entries, both positive and negative, while the other partner gives three things for an entire day. This can be frustrating on both sides. One partner feels like the other is nitpicking the smallest things, and the other partner feels like the lack of effort means they don't really care about the relationship. It's rare to have two people who are going to have similar styles of entries. The story you tell yourself about your partner's inner thoughts and your partner's actual inner thoughts may or may not be accurate. You might be thinking that three entries mean they don't care. In reality, three entries actually might mean they don't feel like sharing it will be well-received. This is something for you to work on as a couple. A long-lasting relationship isn't always a good relationship. Length of time does not equal quality of connection. This challenge can deepen how you understand each other and are able to use your strengths to both add to your love tanks and build a life you design. The goal is to minimize love tank drains, not to avoid telling your partner about love tank drains. There is a huge difference between bottling up inside when your love tank is drained and effectively communicating a drain and then allowing your partner the opportunity to refill the love tank. Let's say your partner drains you with something like the following examples.

- Words of Affirmation → lack of compliments or harsh criticism
- Acts of Service → broken promises or failure to help
- Quality Time → distracted or absent presence
- Physical Touch → withdrawal of affection or touch
- Gifts → forgetting special occasions or giving thoughtless gifts

Sometimes, a partner will drain one love language much more than another. The drain is disproportionate to the refill. One of the worst things you can do as a partner is to not honor the drain or expect more from the fill-up. If your partner says you drained them −$5,000 because you didn't kiss them goodbye before you left for work, when you honor their experience and honesty, that can be very helpful for your relationship. Please don't mock them by saying something like, "Really, because I didn't give you a kiss that drains you $5,000?" Honor their experience, and try your best to get curious. Ask, "Why do you think that drains you so much?" You may be surprised at the answer. Also, the answer may be a very helpful tool in gaining back even more than $5,000 by addressing why they feel that way to begin with. Don't vindictively then subtract $5,000 for the next thing they do to you if it didn't actually drain you the max. Also, don't expect the refill to be the same. If they felt drained $5,000 for you forgetting a goodbye kiss, it might not be the equivalent of the next kiss you give to gain you $5,000. Again, honor their experience.

The best thing you can do for this challenge is to show gratitude that your partner is opening up their inner mind to you. In a world where we could be mind readers, we would know what another person is thinking, but since that isn't our reality, we have to put trust in our partner that they are being honest with us. A way to silence your partner is by mocking their experience and saying something like, "Really, you are going to subtract money for that. That doesn't bother me, so why should it bother you?"

Attention: It is so important to understand that what bothers one partner is almost always not the same intensity as what bothers the other partner, and that is the entire point of this book and challenge.

What is your exchange rate for love tank drains, and why? What in your background happened to drain you so much? If you then address the reason why it was draining in the first place, you may see the value of the drain go down significantly.

This can be an opportunity for a powerful reframe, almost like assigning emotional currency exchange rates to our reactions. Just because something used to cost us $1,000 in emotional energy doesn't mean it has to forever.

Each draining event has:

1. An Emotional Cost (how much it empties your tank now),
2. An Origin Story (why it drains you so deeply), and
3. A Chance for Currency Devaluation (reducing the cost by healing or reframing the origin).

Example: Drain: Your partner forgets to call when they're running late.

Current Emotional Cost: −$2,500 (feels like abandonment, rejection, or like you don't matter).

Visible Reaction: Anger, shutdown, or spiraling thoughts like "they don't prioritize me."

Dig Into the Background (Why It Hurts So Much)

Let's say you grew up with:

- A parent who often broke promises
- No explanation when plans changed
- Emotional unpredictability

Now, "running late without a call" isn't just about time.

It's a trigger for a deeper fear of being forgotten, dismissed, or unimportant.

Active Advanced Preparation

If running late is a trigger for your partner an example of active advance preparation is you prepare a jar of notes on the outside it says, "In case I'm late... and I'm not able to communicate right away that I will be late please know that I love you and I want to get back to you as soon as possible. Pick a note inside to read some of the reasons why I cherish our relationship."

Now let's imagine that you are late and your partner is having an inner voice battle. He's late that means he doesn't care and how could he not take 30 seconds to text me an update that he is running late? Maybe I wouldn't be so mad if my partner would just communicate with me.

Suddenly, the partner who was inside their own head remembers the jar. On the outside it says

"In case I'm late... and I'm not able to communicate right away that I will be late please know that I love you and I want to get back to you as soon as possible."

This calms them and their inner voice down.

Inside the jar is a collection of notes that your partner has never read before. They open one that says, I remember how excited I was on our first date. I knew it was the beginning of something special. I felt a calm sense of comfort around you very early in our relationship and I'm so glad that we picked each other to share our lives with.

This collection of notes may or may not help. But it's certainly worth a try!

Active advanced preparation could be something that you see reflected in your love tank drains and fill ups.

You were late -$500

I read your note and it made me reminisce on our first date it made me feel better +$700

Another half hour went by and I started to get really irritated because now I'm stressed and worried you may have been hurt or killed in a car accident. -$2000

I read another note from the jar +$50. This note didn't mean as much as the first because now my stress level is on high alert and I'm dreading getting a phone call that you are in the hospital after a horrendous car accident and that's why there has been no communication. -$5000 (max)

Instead of spiraling into more negative thoughts I decided to write you a letter while I wait about our first date and all the things I love about you. +$1000

Finally you called, and apologized to me for not communicating sooner. There was no accident so I was relieved you weren't injured. +$5,000 (max)

I told you on the phone that I was able to read two of your notes from the if I'm late jar and I also wrote you a note back. Even though my stomach was in knots while I waited, the experience made me realize that I'm afraid of losing you. I just want to have a wonderful relationship where we get to spend our lives together and I'm scared of our time being cut short by a car accident. +$3000

In detailing the chain of events that happened, the late partner can hopefully see that it's not just about being late without communicating. There are emotions involved that are important to be aware of.

Active advanced preparation like a jar of notes prepped for the just in case I'm not around moments that are specifically around your partner's triggers can have a domino effect and really help to heal your partner's triggers. They don't have to go into a negative thought spiral. Instead, they can use their inner self talk to work on healing their deeply rooted wounds. You can communicate with them when you are unable to do so at the moment. It takes time to create a jar like this but in the moment that your partner is able to use it, you may be grateful after the fact that it was a tool you could both use.

Reframing the Drain

When you see that the $2,500 drain is partly made up of old emotional debt, you can start to do two things:

1. Separate the past from the present:
   "My partner is late. That's inconvenient—but it doesn't mean I'm unloved or unsafe like I once felt."

2. Assign a new exchange rate:
   After healing the wound, you might feel differently about the value you would assign in the future, especially if your partner is able to reassure you in other ways.

As a partner, healing wounds and seeing the drain go down can be a very powerful part of this process. Looking together at the drains and attempting to heal some of them together so that the overall impact of the emotional drains goes down is really transformative for a couple. The way to do this is to honor the amount and how much it is impacting you. As part of the rules, don't change the current valuation of a love tank train, but after a deep conversation, you can acknowledge that if this were to happen again, I would be able to deduct less money. For the purposes of this challenge, the honor system is that once the transaction is recorded, you aren't trying to change the numbers, but you can definitely talk about the numbers and then add money for talking about it.

Asking why your partner is drained so much is extremely powerful. Even more powerful is asking how, in the future, you could alter your behavior so that when this drain is about to happen, you could minimize the damage. It's unlikely that your partner will never run late again, but if they are running late, what can they do to make you feel loved in the process? That is a very powerful dialogue to have with each other!

When to do this challenge: I do not recommend doing this challenge in a relationship that started less than six months ago. New relationship energy is very unique, and I didn't design this challenge for brand-new relationships. I don't think it's productive to start a relationship with this communication style. So, if you have been dating someone for less than six months, you can read the book and work on writing your letters, but I would wait until you cross the six-month mark before beginning the challenge together.

CHAPTER 6

Legacy Love – Investing in Dreams, Modeling Growth, and Giving from the Heart

"True love is not about perfection, but about generosity—the willingness to pour into someone else even when you're still filling your own cup."
— **Unknown**

Investing in Dreams

We often think of wealth in terms of numbers—dollars in the bank, returns on investments, equity in real estate. But there's another kind of wealth that is far more powerful and lasting: emotional wealth.

Are you just putting up with your partner because years or decades earlier, you made a vow to them? Ideally, in a home where you are Relationship Millionaires, you're not just co-existing—you're investing in each other. What dreams do you both have that you can each support? When you have the confidence that your relationship is good, other areas in your life will likely start to flourish as well! That's where emotional wealth multiplies. When you say, "I believe in you," and back it up with your time, encouragement, and effort, your relationship grows exponentially. You're not just being supportive, you're compounding trust. You're giving your partner the freedom to grow—and that is one of the most generous things you can offer.

Even when your dreams are different, you can still look in the same direction. By opening up to each other in this deeper, more transparent way, you are building a future together where both of you feel seen and safe to pursue what lights you up.

And here's where the millionaire mindset meets the heart: emotional generosity is abundance. When you treat your partner with grace—even when they're tired, short-tempered, or scared—you're saying, "There's enough love here to go around. I'm not afraid to give." Just like in business, people who operate from a scarcity mindset hold back. They protect themselves instead of investing. But Relationship Millionaires give love like it will come back with interest—and it does.

Modeling Growth

A note to the parents reading this:

If your child grew up and married someone exactly like you—in how you communicate, show up, give support, handle conflict, and dream— would you feel like they made a good choice?

If the answer makes you pause, think about how you are treating your partner. Let it be your invitation to change. You don't need to be perfect—you just need to be aware. Your children are watching not just how you treat your partner, but how you treat yourself, your growth, and your dreams.

You are shaping the blueprint for your kids' lives and their future relationships. Be the kind of partner you'd want them to have. If you haven't in the past, use this challenge as a fresh slate. Plenty of people declare bankruptcy and come back to be multi-millionaires. It doesn't matter where you start; everyone has the capacity to change.

Be the kind of human you'd want your kids to become. Your kids are watching everything. Since kids are too young to experience a relationship of their own, they have your relationship as the front and center of their young world. Your dynamic becomes their definition. That could be positive or negative, and that's for you to decide. How have you been showing up to set an example? Your tone becomes their inner voice. Your way of handling stress builds their inner world. Their comfort zone is shaped in their younger years.

They're learning love by watching you live it.

So, be mindful. Be kind. Be someone you'd want them to imitate, not recover from.

Be the kind of partner you'd want them to end up with.

Be the kind of human you'd want them to become.

Be intentional about what that blueprint contains in the world of those impressionable who are watching you. In the next chapter, we will talk about building a love map. Think about your legacy and what you want your reputation to be before you build your love map. What is it that you want, and who do you want to be for your partner?

Giving from the Heart

In a relationship, there are two kinds of giving: the transactional kind— "I'll do this if you do that," and the transformational kind—"I give because I love." One builds resentment. The other builds emotional wealth.

Giving from the heart doesn't always look big. Sometimes, it's putting your phone down when your partner starts talking. Sometimes, it's making their coffee before they wake up, picking up the towel they left on the floor, or stepping in without being asked. These may not sound like millionaire moves. But they are. Because every generous act says: I see you. I value you. I choose us.

When you're in the thick of life—especially parenting—it can feel easier to keep score. "I did this, so you should do that." But Relationship Millionaires keep different books. They don't give to get. They give to grow. They know that love isn't measured in fairness, but in overflow. And that kind of giving multiplies.

Emotional generosity also means choosing grace when your partner falls short. It's choosing softness over hurtful sarcasm. Choosing curiosity over criticism. It's saying, "I know you're trying, and I'm here," even if it's been a hard day. Even if you're tired, too.

One of the richest investments you can make is to give when it would be easier to withdraw. To reach when you feel like retreating. That's what keeps the account full. That's what models abundance.

Your children will grow up watching not just what you give, but how you give. They'll learn if love is about keeping tabs or about being tuned in. They'll internalize whether love comes with conditions or compassion. They'll mirror what you model.

So give with joy. Give from the heart, not because you owe it to anyone, but because you know that giving without expectation builds amazing relationships. That's what makes you a true Relationship Millionaire.

CHAPTER 7

Advice from Relationship Experts

"In a good relationship, people get angry, but in a very different way. The Marriage Masters see a problem a bit like a soccer ball. They kick it around. It's 'our' problem." — **John M. Gottman**

There is real wisdom in the work of professionals, and I don't want to downplay their training, experience, or value. But I've learned that if you don't have the extra funds to comfortably invest in therapy, reading books written by therapists is an incredibly powerful alternative. It's a far better use of your time and energy than doing nothing—and it's often free.

If you can afford both? Amazing. Do both. There's nothing quite like one-on-one support. But if you're already tight on money and behind on bills, paying for therapy may actually create more stress. Fortunately, there's another way: You can walk into your local library, head to the relationships section, and check out a book that could completely change the way you see your partner.

I've outlined some interesting relationship books and a short summary. These are only a few; there are tons of additional relationship books that are really great.

Here are six powerful reads to help you build emotional wealth, deepen your connection, and communicate like your relationship is your most valuable investment—because it is.

* * *

1. The Seven Principles for Making Marriage Work

Author: John Gottman, Ph.D.

Quote:

"Happy marriages are based on a deep friendship."

Summary:

Based on decades of research, this book lays out seven practical principles that help couples thrive. Gottman teaches how to build love maps, manage conflict with empathy, and strengthen emotional connection through small, everyday moments. It's like marriage therapy in book form—with step-by-step guidance to protect and repair your relationship.

2. Talk to Me Like I'm Someone You Love

Author: Nancy Dreyfus, Psy.D.

Quote:

"I need you to say what you feel, not what you think I want to hear."

Summary:

This book offers real, usable phrases for when you're too upset to think straight. With over 100 emotional flashcards and healing scripts, it helps couples say the hard things in a way that opens hearts instead of shutting them down. Ideal for those moments when you want to reconnect but don't have the words.

3. Getting the Love You Want

Author: Harville Hendrix, Ph.D.

Quote:

"Conflict is growth trying to happen."

Summary:

Harville Hendrix explores why we're drawn to certain partners—and why our relationships often reflect unresolved childhood wounds. With the Imago Dialogue and other exercises, this book helps couples transform blame into curiosity and triggers into healing. It's perfect for those ready to do the deep inner work of conscious love.

4. The Relationship Cure

Author: John Gottman, Ph.D.

Quote:

"A bid for connection is any attempt to get attention, affection, and support from your partner."

Summary:

While Gottman's marriage book focuses on couples, this one zooms out to include all relationships. It centers around the concept of "bids for connection"—those little ways we say, "Notice me." Learning to recognize and respond to those bids can strengthen your bond faster than grand gestures ever could.

5. Loving Bravely

Author: Alexandra H. Solomon, Ph.D.

Quote:

"The foundation of a strong relationship is your ability to know yourself, soothe yourself, and speak your truth."

Summary:

This is a must-read for anyone who wants to stop repeating old patterns and start showing up in love with confidence and clarity. Solomon blends psychology, mindfulness, and self-reflection to help readers love from a place of wholeness. If you're doing the emotional work of becoming a Relationship Millionaire, this book is a mirror and a map.

6. The 5 Love Languages

Author: Gary Chapman

Quote:

"People tend to criticize their spouse most loudly in the area where they themselves have the deepest emotional need."

Summary:

You've probably heard of this one—and for good reason. It simplifies something we often overcomplicate: the way we give and receive love. Whether it's Words of Affirmation, Acts of Service, Receiving Gifts, Quality Time, or Physical Touch, knowing your partner's love language is like having a cheat code for connection. This book is a reminder that love is not just a feeling—it's a skill.

The Rhythm of Love: Harmony, Disharmony, Repair

Let's talk about what real love looks like in the day-to-day. Not the Instagram highlight reel kind of love—but the kind where your partner forgets to do something you asked, you snap a little too quickly, or you both feel distant and don't know how to say it out loud.

Esther Perel teaches that every relationship moves in a rhythm: harmony, disharmony, and repair. It's not a failure when disharmony shows up—it's part of the cycle. That shift from "we're good" to "ugh, what's going on?" is something every couple experiences. What matters is not avoiding that middle space, but how quickly and honestly we get to the repair.

You know those little tensions? The sigh when one partner forgets to load the dishwasher. The silence in the car after a disagreement. The feeling that you're in different worlds, even though you're in the same room. That's disharmony. And it doesn't mean the love is broken. It means you're human.

The million-dollar skill is in how we repair.

Repair doesn't have to be a grand gesture. Sometimes, it's a text that says, "I didn't like how we left that conversation. Can we try again?" Or a hand resting on your partner's back, just saying, "I'm still here." Or even a joke that makes you both laugh again. The goal isn't perfection—it's reconnection.

Think about it like this: if your emotional connection is a bank account, every kind gesture, inside joke, or "just thinking of you" moment is a deposit. Every sharp word, eye roll, or forgotten promise is a withdrawal. Disharmony happens when the balance dips. Repair is what brings it back up.

Perel says that repair is not about being right, it's about returning to us. It's saying, "I value this connection more than I value winning this argument." That's relationship wealth. That's a millionaire mindset applied to love.

So ask yourself gently: *How do we repair? Do we go quiet and pretend nothing happened? Do we blow it up and move on too fast? Or do we have a real, caring moment where we acknowledge the crack and mend it with intention?*

Relationship millionaires don't avoid disharmony. They expect it. And they develop tools—like the ones in this challenge—to move through it with grace and respect.

Harmony is where love thrives and where you want to be as often as possible. Disharmony is where it requires action to get back to harmony. What is standing in your way... repair. But what repair technique should you use? You don't want to put a metaphorical band-aid on a bullet hole. The relationship cash register is meant to be a tool to help you gauge the depth of the disharmony because, with words, it could feel like a deep cut that requires a trip to urgent care, but to your partner, it's not that big of a deal and is a paper cut. Using numbers, you can gauge and see whether your repair actually repaired and refilled your partner's love tank.

Maybe you need to do more than one thing to repair. It helps to have numbers to calculate where you are right now. Harmony is positive interactions; disharmony is negative ones. Repair is a positive interaction, but repairing a negative situation. It doesn't always have to be a direct repair. Sometimes, a handwritten note can be the repair for something, and the note has nothing to do with what happened! Sometimes, your partner's love tank gets filled by something that isn't the same as what drained it.

When my husband and I were going through natural cycles of harmony, disharmony, and repair, we thought the disharmony was a real problem. We didn't realize how to create a natural flow between the three. Our repair skills were based on the tools we used when we first started dating, and they weren't working. Once we were in a 15-year relationship, we needed to upgrade our toolbox to get some more avenues to repair. That didn't happen overnight, but it did eventually happen. Disharmony didn't feel good, but with more tools, we were able to navigate through it better. Harmony was easier to get back to because we had better repair tools. Also, the disharmony didn't feel so threatening or last as long.

I hope that this book is an added tool for those who have any struggle with moving from disharmony to repair and back to harmony. I congratulate you on having an open mind and getting this far in the book to give this tool a chance.

I often wonder if there are divorces that happen because this cycle gets to a point where the couple is lacking the tools to get from disharmony to repair and back to harmony. They love each other, and they have a solid foundation, but they find themselves toggling between disharmony and failed attempts at repair. My hope for you is that this book is not your only tool. It is one tool, but there are a lot of other tools that can also help!

When my relationship was struggling, I turned to Dr. John Gottman for insights. His advice helped me understand how to rebuild connections and improve communication.

The Magic Ratio: Dr. John Gottman

Dr. Gottman's research emphasizes the importance of maintaining a 5:1 ratio—five positive interactions for every one negative interaction. Relationships that dip below this threshold often face strain, while those exceeding it thrive. Restoring a healthy ratio requires intentional effort but offers immense rewards.

With the relationship cash register, couples can tangibly track their progress toward achieving the magic ratio. For example:

- Positive interactions, such as compliments, affectionate gestures, or small acts of kindness, earn relationship dollars.
- Negative interactions, like criticism or moments of neglect, deduct dollars.

The difficult part of a relationship is that the negative comments hurt more and stand out more in your memory. Even if you have a 5:1 ratio, the five positive things often slip away into your memories, and the one thing that hurts stands out so much more. The repair is difficult when the same thing keeps hurting you over and over again. It's hard to focus on the positive when the negative hurts so bad. This challenge is one that quantifies the positive and hopefully can help both you and your partner feel like their negative actions do not have to hold a controlling position in their mind. If the love tank gets drained, and then the love tank is filled back up, you can both attempt to release that hurt from your memory.

When someone does something to subtract from the other partner's love tank, both love tanks frequently get drained. Getting news that you drained your partner is almost always also draining for the partner who did something to upset their partner. Whether intentionally or unintentionally, if you are in a healthy relationship, you care about your partner's feelings. That might not always come across to your partner, but at the core of a relationship, your partner's feelings matter. That moment becomes an invitation: not to spiral into guilt or defense, but to lean in with empathy. That is what the core of this challenge can help with. A negative interaction is an invitation to do thoughtful things to fill your partner's love tank. It doesn't have to be directly making up for the thing that you disagreed about. The beauty of this system is that you can have one action drain the love tank, and instead of trying to directly make up for what you did wrong, you can show your partner you love them in other ways.

This does not give you a free pass to do hurtful things and then make up for it with other things. Please always try your best to avoid draining your partner's love tank. But don't avoid draining their love tank at the expense of who you truly are.

For example, a couple has a new baby, and their love tank is being drained constantly. Sleep-deprived and recovering from childbirth, one partner didn't pick up the medicine from the pharmacy on their way home, even though they were reminded twice. They come home and realize they forgot to stop at the pharmacy. It's natural for a love tank to get drained in this moment, but it doesn't mean that there isn't compassion and understanding that a new baby brings a lot of added pressure and stress. In a traditional way of life, the partner who forgot to stop at the pharmacy feels bad, as if they let their partner down. Sometimes, it's worse for the partner who forgot and more draining on the partner who doesn't want to feel like they aren't pulling their weight in the relationship. Imagine this interaction.

Partner A: Hey, did you pick up the medicine from the pharmacy?

Partner B: Oh my goodness, I was so focused on getting home to you and the baby, I completely forgot.

Partner A: This drained my love tank.

Partner B: I feel like a complete idiot.

Partner A: It's okay, would you mind going back out to pick up the medicine?

Partner B: Yes, of course, I can. How about I take the baby with me and you put on a guided meditation while I'm gone?

Partner A: That would be really nice.

Partner B: I just feel like a total idiot that I rushed home and forgot when you reminded me twice not to forget to stop on my way home.

Partner A: It's alright.

Partner B: I'll pick up your favorite type of mixed nuts.

In the traditional world, that interaction could happen without any monetary values being placed. However, in the world of placing monetary values, I want to take this opportunity to point out how this interaction can go two different ways.

Money Calculation 1

Partner A: You forgot my medication, it's no big deal, −$20.

Partner B: I feel like an idiot. Can I take the baby with me and set up a guided meditation for you?

Partner A: That is so thoughtful of you, +$1,000.

If Partner A is being honest, then Partner B leaves for the store feeling like they have more than made up for forgetting the medication.

Partner A: When you came home with my favorite type of mixed nuts, that meant a lot, +$5,000.

Partner B feels great and validated that they are $5,980 in the positive.

The following is the same event, but the reaction, since we are all reacting subjectively, is different. We should aim to be as honest as we can with our feelings, not what we think the amount should be according to society, but our own true feelings. All feelings are valid, and you should try to award and subtract money based on your own personal feelings.

Money Calculation 2

Partner A: You forgot my medication. I've been in pain all day, and having to be in pain longer really drains my love tank, −$5,000.

Partner B: I feel like an idiot. Can I take the baby with me and set up a guided meditation for you?

Partner A: Sure, but a guided mediation isn't going to eliminate my pain, +$100.

Partner B: Is there anything else I can pick up from the store to make you feel better?

Partner A: No, thanks, just the medicine.

Partner B leaves for the store knowing that their partner is in the negative love tank. I'm glad partner A was honest in this scenario because that leads to an honest and open relationship. If one person says it's no big deal when really they are in immense pain, that's not helpful. So, partner B has some more work to do.

Partner A: When you came home with my favorite type of mixed nuts, that was nice, +$500.

Partner B is still in the negative $4,400.

In a lot of toxic patterns, Partner B could get defensive at this point because they are negative $4,400, and they pick a fight and point out the things that they have done and didn't get credit for, and the faults of Partner A.

As a whole, that drains everyone's love tanks more and more. This happens a lot in relationships. Our bodies are meant to protect us, and if we feel threatened that we are in the negative, our hormones can really get in the way.

Partner B: How about I give you a massage?

Partner A: That would be nice, +$2,000.

Partner B: How about you get to pick the movie we watch tonight?

Partner A: I've really been wanting to watch this movie. Thanks for letting me pick, +$3,000.

Now, partner B is $600 in the positive. Should they stop there being in the positive, or do they want to go above and beyond to not just be in the green but have a cushion in the green?

Partner B decides to write a love note on how excited they are to start this new parenting journey and how amazing a parent they know their partner is going to be.

Partner A: That love note made me cry, and it was so beautiful, +$5,000.

Now, partner B is fully feeling like they filled up their partner's love tank and didn't just do the bare minimum.

Note from the author: You don't need numbers to do this and to live life. But my argument is that words alone don't have a way to gauge a love tank as concretely as numbers do. In a car, on the dashboard, it says X miles until empty. That is concrete data that continues to go down until you go to the gas station to fill up. If your car said you have some gas left, you wouldn't know if "some" meant 100 miles left or 10 miles left. The word some is subjective. If you told 50 people this car has some gas left in the tank and asked, "How many miles do you think it can go?" You would get a lot of different answers. If you say this gas meter says it has 15 miles left to go, all 50 people would have a number to go by. If you had a car and your gas gauge meter was broken, it would be hard for you to know how much gas you have left. At first, if life were just one interaction, you could monitor it, but life is a web of interactions and external pressures that numbers allow for you to keep track of and make it easier to fill more than you drain.

Even if it doesn't always come across clearly, in strong relationships, your partner's feelings matter to you, not as a burden, but as a compass. That mutual care is the heartbeat of a relationship that can weather any obstacle. The answer isn't avoiding obstacles, it's navigating the inevitable obstacles.

Using this system, you can see if your daily balance reflects a positive-to-negative interaction ratio. If you notice a pattern of red days, it may signal a need to increase intentional acts of connection.

Gottman also highlights the importance of responding to **bids for connection**, small moments when your partner seeks attention or support. Missing these bids or dismissing them can create emotional distance, while recognizing and responding to them strengthens trust and affection.

The Role of Desire and Connection: Esther Perel

Esther Perel emphasizes the tension between stability and novelty in long-term relationships. She describes how couples often struggle to balance the security of familiarity with the excitement of mystery and desire. Perel writes, "Love rests on two pillars: surrender and autonomy. Our need for togetherness exists alongside our need for separateness."

This idea can be integrated into the relationship cash register by assigning value to actions that build both stability and excitement. For example:

- Stability can be fostered through consistent acts of care, like sharing a meal or engaging in a comforting routine, earning relationship dollars that reflect dependability.
- Novelty can be created through surprises, spontaneous adventures, or trying something new together, which earns relationship dollars that reflect variety and excitement.

Perel also discusses the importance of curiosity in relationships. Rather than assuming you already know everything about your partner, she suggests approaching your relationship with a sense of wonder and discovery. By updating your **Love Maps**, as Gottman suggests, and incorporating curiosity, couples can create a sense of renewal and growth within their partnership.

Growth and Contribution: Tony Robbins

Tony Robbins teaches that relationships flourish when both partners commit to growth and contribution. He outlines six human needs that drive all behavior:

1. **Certainty:** The need for stability and predictability.
2. **Variety:** The need for novelty and excitement.
3. **Significance:** The need to feel valued and important.
4. **Love and Connection:** The need for meaningful relationships.
5. **Growth:** The need for personal development.
6. **Contribution:** The need to give and serve beyond oneself.

Robbins explains that relationships thrive when both partners strive to meet these needs for each other. The relationship cash register can help couples assess whether they are meeting these needs. For instance:

- A partner who values **certainty** might appreciate acts of service, like organizing the household, which could earn $1,500 relationship dollars. A partner that values variety over certainty might give that same act $300.

- A partner who craves **variety** might respond more strongly to spontaneous surprises, like a date night, which could earn $2,000 relationship dollars. A partner who values certainty might subtract money for this event because they had other plans, and this surprise date night just got in the way. Two things can be true at the same time. In this case, a partner can appreciate the effort of the surprise date night and give positive $150, they can also deduct money because they were planning to watch a playoff basketball game that they have been looking forward to for years, −$500. Being honest about your love tank at first may be difficult. In the long run, this challenge can help build better communication. Maybe it's circumstantial. On any other night, you would love this surprise date night; however, the team you root for hasn't been in the playoffs in five years, and you've been really looking forward to this game.

Very important note from the author: There are times when your love tank is about to be drained, and there are times when your love tank is already drained. In this instance, the playoff game hasn't happened yet. There is time for a solution that drains everyone's love tanks to a minimum. Being honest with each other about how much your love tank is about to be draining in the event that something happens can be very valuable information. If you want to watch a playoff basketball game that you have been waiting for 5 years to see. You could ask your partner, is it possible to do your date night tomorrow night instead of tonight because I'd really like to watch the playoff game live.

By intentionally aligning actions with your partner's top needs, you foster growth and contribution within the relationship.

Using the Relationship Cash Register to Measure Progress

The relationship cash register provides a tangible way to combine these expert insights:

- Use Dr. Gottman's **magic ratio** to track whether your daily balance reflects more positive than negative interactions.
- Incorporate Esther Perel's emphasis on balancing stability and novelty by assigning value to actions that build both.
- Apply Tony Robbins' six human needs to ensure your actions align with what truly fulfills your partner.

Overcoming Common Challenges

1. **Feeling Disconnected:**
   - Start small by building up positive interactions and responding to bids for connection.
   - Use the relationship cash register to quantify efforts and visualize progress.

2. **Poor Communication:**
   - Begin difficult conversations gently, focusing on solutions rather than blame.
   - Incorporate curiosity and mutual understanding to navigate differences.

3. **Loss of Intimacy:**
   - Prioritize small moments of affection and find opportunities to create shared adventures.
   - Balance the need for stability with the excitement of novelty to rekindle desire.

Closing Thoughts

As Esther Perel says, "The quality of our relationships determines the quality of our lives." By applying the principles of Gottman, Robbins, and Perel, and integrating them with the relationship cash register, couples can transform their connection into one rich with trust, passion, and joy.

Through intentional effort and measurable progress, you can create a relationship that not only meets your needs but exceeds your dreams— building a partnership that truly makes you Relationship Millionaires together.

CHAPTER 8

Grace in Relationships: A Fresh Start Every Day

"Each morning we are born again. What we do today is what matters most." — **Buddha**

In every relationship, challenges and imperfections are inevitable. But the beauty of love lies in the opportunity to begin again—every single day. Grace allows us to choose understanding over judgment, presence over resentment, and growth over perfection.

Great relationships aren't built by perfect people. They're built by two imperfect partners committed to growing together, with compassion, intentionality, and gratitude. When you wake up each day with the mindset that your relationship deserves a fresh start, you create space for emotional healing and long-term connection.

The Power of Grace

Grace is a gift—not something we earn, but something we choose to offer. In relationships, grace means recognizing your partner's flaws without punishing them for being human. It means responding to mistakes with love, not silence or shame. It doesn't mean accepting poor behavior without accountability—but it does mean staying grounded in kindness, even during conflict.

Sometimes, relationships break because one or both partners stop believing repair is possible. This challenge is about finding out if that repair is possible—and whether you can rebuild from a place of love and shared responsibility.

When someone does something to subtract from their partner's love tank, both partners feel the drain. And here's the truth: even the partner who made the mistake is usually hurt by that disconnection. In healthy relationships, your partner's feelings matter—even when you fall short.

A Fresh Start Every Day

Every morning is a blank slate. You and your partner can choose to carry yesterday's weight... or you can choose renewal.

Your mindset sets the tone. When you expect joy, connection, and kindness, your brain begins to filter the world through that lens. That's not wishful thinking—it's neuroscience.

The Psychology of Positivity: How Your Brain Works in Love

Confirmation Bias

Your brain is wired to seek out what you already believe. If you expect your partner to let you down, you'll see every small misstep as evidence. But if you expect kindness, effort, and good intentions—you'll notice those things more.

Here's how to train your brain toward love:

1. Start with Gratitude

Begin each day by thinking of three things you appreciate about your partner. Share them out loud. Reward each other with "relationship dollars" when this habit becomes part of your daily rhythm.

2. Reframe Challenges

Instead of viewing an argument as a failure, see it as an invitation to grow closer. In fact, when your partner brings up a concern (even if it's uncomfortable), thank them for the vulnerability. You might even reward that honesty.

Avoiding issues doesn't create peace—it builds quiet resentment.

But here's the nuance: There's a fine line between not sweating the small stuff and suppressing valuable communication. Ask yourself:

- Am I letting this go because it truly doesn't matter?
- Or am I afraid to bring it up because I don't want to rock the boat?

If it's the latter, write it down—even if you end up assigning it a "–$.01" in your relationship ledger. This shows your partner that it mattered enough to acknowledge, but not enough to cause conflict. That tiny subtraction can actually build trust and transparency.

3. Celebrate Small Wins

Don't be stingy. Acknowledge the little things—text messages, shared laughs, cleaning up after the kids. Reward generously. Confidence grows in an atmosphere of appreciation.

The Science of Seeing the Good

Research shows that couples who intentionally focus on each other's positive traits experience higher levels of satisfaction, emotional security, and intimacy. This doesn't mean ignoring real problems—it means balancing truth with appreciation.

Appreciating Your Partner: A Daily Practice

- See what's right. Notice even the smallest positive actions.
- Say it out loud. "Thank you for doing that." "I love how you handled that." "I noticed—and I appreciate it."

- Celebrate the fact they're still here. They've chosen to stay. That in itself is powerful.

The Danger of Silent Resentment

Some people believe that avoiding conflict keeps the peace in a relationship. But keeping irritations to yourself—just to keep the peace—actually weakens the relationship. The goal isn't to be conflict-free. The goal is to communicate quickly, clearly, and with grace.

The healthiest couples don't avoid issues. They address them lovingly and let them go.

Walking Away Is Always an Option

And that's exactly why choosing to stay matters.

If you're still here—still reading, still engaging—pause and honor that. You're making the conscious choice to try. That decision alone is worth celebrating.

Ask yourself:

- Why am I still here?

Extending Grace for the Negative

Your partner will disappoint you. You will disappoint them. Grace means:

- Separating actions from intentions.
- Focusing on the bigger picture.
- Forgiving freely—not because you forget, but because you choose to heal.

Clarity Matters

Grace does not mean tolerating disrespect. It means communicating clearly and compassionately when something needs to change.

Try saying:

- "I feel more connected when we talk before bed."
- "I appreciate when you check in during the day—it makes me feel remembered."

Then, set small goals. Celebrate progress. Let your love evolve in the light of grace.

Practical Daily Exercises

1. Morning Gratitude Practice:
   Write down three things you appreciate about your partner. I strongly encourage you to share your morning gratitude with what you are specifically grateful for about your partner, and award each other money to reinforce this habit. I've read so many growth books that point to magic happening when you begin a morning gratitude ritual. Let that magic shine through your relationship!

2. Reset Ritual:
   Create a daily reset—coffee together, a hug, a kiss goodbye. Something that anchors you.

3. Weekly Appreciation Date:
   Pick a night to reflect on what you've appreciated about each other and where you'd like to grow. Don't be afraid to directly ask each other what you can do this week to show your love. Your partner isn't a mind reader. Giving them some ideas of what you want is a huge help. Don't be upset if they don't do

them right away, but keep the requests coming. Remember, change rarely happens overnight. Don't let a few instances of missed requests make you think it's not worth your time to keep making requests. Keep asking and keep offering loving actions towards your partner! Use these weekly appreciation times to really reflect on the past week and make your requests for the following week crystal clear.

Real-Life Inspiration

One couple transformed their marriage by simply listing five things they loved about each other every night. Another kept a "Reset Jar" filled with loving actions or affirmations—drawing one whenever tension arose.

Grace doesn't require grand gestures. It thrives in consistency.

Closing Thoughts on This Chapter

Grace is a powerful tool for building a thriving relationship. It allows you to see your partner's humanity, embrace their imperfections, and focus on their strengths.

By starting fresh each day, cultivating a positive outlook, and addressing challenges with clarity, you can create a relationship rooted in love, trust, and appreciation.

Remember, every day is a new opportunity to grow together. Choose grace, choose gratitude, and choose each other—every single day.

CHAPTER 9

Repair Rituals & Relationship Energy

"Peace is not the absence of conflict, but the ability to cope with it." — **Mahatma Gandhi**

L ove is energy. Mistakes are inevitable. But your rituals—those sacred little resets—are what transform relationship breakdowns into breakthroughs.

When we hurt each other, it isn't always intentional—but it's always felt. The nervous system holds onto emotional friction, and unless it's cleared, it begins to stack.

Over time, these unprocessed energetic drains deplete your emotional bank account, and couples start to feel more like adversaries than teammates.

Your Energy Is Physiological

You don't just feel drained after a fight—your body actually is.

Conflict triggers your fight or flight response, floods you with cortisol, and drops your ability to connect. You might go numb, shut down, or lash out—not because you're bad, but because your system is overloaded.

That's why repair rituals matter. They're not just sweet gestures.

They're somatic resets—body-based signals to tell your nervous system:

"We're safe. We're loved. It's okay to reconnect."

And the best part? It doesn't take long.

Energy can be restored in just a few intentional moments.

The Mistake Ritual Toolbox

When you or your partner makes a mistake, have a few rituals ready. You don't have to use the same one every time. Just do something to reset the energy.

Try one of these:

- Special Snack: Go-to comfort food or shared treat you both love.
- 1-Minute Hug: No words, just connection.
- 5-Minute Make-Out Session: Shift the energy with intimacy.
- Slow Dance to a Song: Pick a song now that becomes your reset anthem.
- The Mistake Jar: Drop three slips of paper in the jar when you make a mistake. Each slip contains a surprise ritual. Pick one and do it, even if you don't feel like it. Afterwards, award or deduct money depending on how it shifted the energy.

Energetic Accounting: How Love Tanks Really Work

Mistakes don't just cause tension—they drain love tanks. But the way you acknowledge the drain matters just as much as the drain itself.

Each person is responsible for tracking their own love tank balance, and it's okay to say, "That moment took something out of me." The Relationship Millionaire system allows for emotional deductions, but those must be done with respect, not shame.

Here's the critical difference:

Example 1: Invalidation (What Not to Do)

Alex subtracts $100 after feeling dismissed during a conversation.

Their partner, Jamie, is frustrated that they didn't feel like they acted dismissively:

"Are you seriously going to subtract money for that? That's ridiculous."

What just happened?

Jamie invalidated Alex's emotional truth. That response is a secondary drain.

It says: "Your experience is not real."

This creates more distance and often escalates the tension.

Example 2: Simultaneous Drain (What's Okay)

Alex subtracts $100.

Jamie expressed they they are drained by the experience of being told they are acting dismissive and also subtracts $50.

What's the difference?

Jamie isn't invalidating Alex. They're just acknowledging they were drained, too.

Now, both partners can see the numbers and recognize:

"Wow, that moment cost us both something. Let's repair this."

You both are allowed to feel hurt. You both are allowed to subtract.

Just don't make each other feel bad for deducting money and participating in the challenge.

Energetic Awareness Tip:

Sometimes, one person is still holding on to something, and the other has moved on.

You may feel tempted to say:

"Are you really still upset about that?"

Instead, try:

"I see you're still feeling it. What can we do to shift the energy?"

Because here's the truth:

Repair rituals are not just for the person who made the mistake—they're for both people.

Leave Blank Space for Your Rituals

Use the spaces below to co-create your own rituals. These don't have to be big or serious.

In fact, the best rituals are the ones that make you both smile through the tension.

Your Go-To Reset Rituals:

_____

_____

_____

_____

_____

_____

_____

_____

Final Word: Love Is Energy

You are allowed to mess up. You are allowed to feel off.

But you are also responsible for what you do next.

When you feel the drain, respond with intention.

Rebuild trust.

Restore energy.

Repair the bond.

Because Relationship Millionaires don't avoid mistakes.

They just know how to bounce back—together.

CHAPTER 10

Encouragement to Have Fun with the Challenge

"Play is the highest form of research."
— **Albert Einstein**

L et's talk about fun. Yes, fun—the thing that often gets lost somewhere between paying bills, parenting, and juggling life's endless responsibilities. But here's the thing: If your relationship isn't filled with joy, laughter, and playful moments, what's the point? Building a great relationship shouldn't feel like work all the time. This challenge is about more than just improving your connection—it's about rediscovering the simple, lighthearted joy of being together.

When we first fall in love, fun comes so naturally. It's the late-night adventures, the inside jokes, the silly things we do just to make the other person smile. But over time, life gets heavier, and those spontaneous moments can fade. This chapter is here to remind you that the journey to becoming relationship millionaires isn't just about reaching the $1,000,000 mark. It's about creating a million-dollar experience along the way.

The Power of Play

Research shows that play isn't just for kids—it's essential for adults, too. Playfulness can reduce stress, build trust, and reignite the spark in your relationship. Whether it's a board game, a silly dance in the kitchen, or an impromptu karaoke session, moments of play bring you closer. They remind you that your partner isn't just your co-parent, roommate, or life teammate—they're your favorite person to share a laugh with.

Make It Personal

The key to having fun with this challenge is to personalize it. What makes you and your partner laugh until your cheeks hurt? What activities bring out your inner child? Maybe it's something as simple as a movie night where you both pick your favorite childhood films. Or maybe it's a bit of friendly competition—playing a game of ping-pong. The beauty of this challenge is that it's as unique as the two of you.

Celebrate the Small Wins

You don't have to wait until you hit the $1,000,000 mark to celebrate. In fact, now it's time to set up two mini checkpoints along the way.

- $100,000 mini-reward when you open your letter.
- $500,000 mini-reward when you open your letter.

I encourage you to celebrate these checkpoints along the way. These small celebrations keep the challenge exciting and reinforce the idea that progress matters just as much as the end goal.

Bring in the Element of Surprise

One of the best ways to keep the challenge fun is to incorporate surprises. Leave a note in their lunchbox, plan a mystery date, or show up with their favorite treat for no reason at all. Surprises don't have to be extravagant—they just have to be thoughtful.

Remember Why You Started

When you're feeling tired or overwhelmed, take a step back and remind yourself why you started this journey. You're here because you love each other and because you want your relationship to thrive. The $1,000,000 goal is about so much more than just a number. It's about building a partnership that feels abundant in every way—emotionally, spiritually, and even playfully.

Fun Is the Shortcut to Connection

Here's the magic of fun: It's an instant connector. When you're laughing together, you're not worrying about the stresses of the day or the to-do list for tomorrow. You're present. You're together. And those moments are priceless.

Journaling Prompt:

What is the most fun memory you've shared with your partner? How can you recreate that feeling during this challenge?

_____

_____

_____

Action Plan:

Write down three fun activities you'd like to do together in the next week.

Partner 1

1._____

_____

2._____

_____

3._____

_____

Partner 2

1._____

_____

2._____

_____

3._____

_____

Commit to making one spontaneous, playful gesture toward your partner this week.

CHAPTER 11

Why I Wrote This Book

"To laugh often and much; to win the respect of intelligent people and the affection of children; to earn the appreciation of honest critics and endure the betrayal of false friends; to appreciate beauty, to find the best in others; to leave the world a bit better, whether by a healthy child, a garden patch or a redeemed social condition; to know even one life has breathed easier because you have lived—this is to have succeeded." — **Ralph Waldo Emerson**

I didn't write this book because I had it all figured out. I wrote it because I wanted to figure out a better way with the person I love. I wrote it because I felt like there are probably other people in similar situations to me who love their partner but don't share their first love language. New relationship energy is very powerful, and a long-term relationship and commitment often fall into the monotonous routine of life. I wanted something to change up the day-to-day routines, so there is room to make improvements!

I found there are a lot of people who walk away from relationships they actually want to keep—they just don't have the tools to fix what feels broken. I want to create tools for those couples, and this book is my first tool. I have a lot of other ideas for more tool ideas as well that I hope to create in the future. This is the first of many, and I'm so glad that whoever is reading this book took the time to read it to the end. Writing a book is taking a piece of myself and giving it to you. I'm glad you decided to receive my effort.

If anyone reading this book has a podcast or a stage for me to share my insights and message, I'm happy for you to contact me. You can send me an email at dinamoench@gmail.com.

This book came from me thinking about how everyone receives and gives love differently. I knew I wanted improvements in my ability for more communication, and my mind came up with this system. For anyone who took the time to read this book and doesn't love it, I encourage you to give it a shot if your partner wants to do it. Giving them the gift of seeing inside your brain and feeling confident that your inner world is being shared can do wonders for some love styles. This isn't a permanent way of communicating. You don't continue to share your thoughts forever by giving and subtracting relationship dollars for the rest of your lives. It's a snapshot of your relationship. A challenge that, once completed, can make you and your partner feel like relationship millionaires.

I wrote this for the couples who want their love to last not just in theory, but in the way they live, give, argue, forgive, and begin again—daily. I hope that you find usefulness in the tool that I have provided! I hope more and more people create more and more tools, and that eventually our younger generations are brought up in secure attachment styles, so their journeys to harmonious relationships can be smoother.

It's not about not fighting or not disagreeing; being in a solid relationship is more about knowing that your partner is sharing their inner self and that you are able to have healthy conflict.

If one couple breathes easier after reading this... if one child sees their parents reconnect and feel safe again... if one person feels seen and supported in their effort to love better—then this book was worth the effort it took me to write.

Our Impact on Future Generations of Children

My wish for your children and mine is that they grow up surrounded by a greater focus on emotional wealth. I hope they see love not as something that's given only when things are easy, but as something worth working for, worth investing in, and worth growing through.

When you commit to this Relationship Millionaires challenge, you're not just building connections for yourselves. You're shaping what the children of the world see and will come to expect from love, what they'll normalize in partnership, and what they'll seek and tolerate when it's their turn to choose a teammate in life.

Children are always watching. They absorb how adults resolve conflict. They remember how often you laugh. They notice whether affection is part of your rhythm or reserved for special occasions. And over time, they build a quiet but powerful internal blueprint for their own relationships.

So let them see that love is more than survival and show them the joy and fun involved in relationships. Let them see that commitment doesn't mean perfection; instead, it means intentional loving and understanding that no human is perfect. Let them see some flaws and the rhythm behind harmony, disharmony, repair, and reconnect. Let them see that two imperfect people can learn how to be emotionally generous with one another and build something extraordinary.

If that's the example they grow up with, they won't have to start from scratch. They'll start with a head start. That's emotional inheritance, and it may be the most valuable thing we ever leave behind. If my book is able to help future generations of relationships, I would be so grateful for the ability to play a small part.

Relationships are the most valuable human connection we have. We don't place enough emphasis on the reality that disharmony is going to show up, and we need tools to deal with it. Our future generations can benefit from seeing the disharmony and the repair process, so they can see that conflict is a healthy part of relationships. Conflict isn't meant to be avoided. The Relationship Millionaires book is designed to show that it is unlikely for a couple to be honest and go from $0 to $1,000,000 without deductions. If a couple did that, they would likely be hiding some of their feelings. It's natural to have negative interactions, and it's important for the positive interactions to outweigh the negative interactions. As a whole, beautiful relationships have healthy conflict where respect for your partner's feelings matters to both partners.

This is my hope to help the world be a little better. I hope my kids, grandkids, great-grandkids, and many future generations can read this and get to know a piece of my heart. I hope that kids can see thriving relationships where solid communication is prioritized.

Please share your success stories with me at dinamoench@gmail.com!

Thank you for letting it be part of your journey!

CHAPTER 12

My Wish for You

"The best gift you can give someone is your time, because when you give your time, you are giving a portion of your life that you will never get back."
— **Anonymous**

When I first started writing this book, I told myself, *If even one couple's marriage improves because of this, I will be amazed!* My mind wonders whether a couple really starts from $0 and makes it all the way to $1,000,000, and if they do, will they say afterwards that their communication improved? If they do, I will be so happy.

An improved relationship and success stories are what I dream about as I write this book. It's about the quiet moments behind the scenes. The way you hold each other's hands in hard seasons. The way your children look to you and learn what love looks like. The way your home feels when you choose kindness, again and again.

My wish for you is that this book becomes more than just pages on a shelf. I hope it becomes part of your story. I hope it becomes a mirror for the moments that you look on that matter most—the ones that no one else sees, but that build your emotional fortune day by day. This gives you a record for the time you do it, and years from now, you can look back on a and reminisce and hopefully laugh at the silly moments and see how far you improved over time.

I hope you and your partner laugh louder. That you fight fairer. That you learn to pause before reacting. That you come back to repair more quickly. That you tell each other what they do right more often than what they do to upset you. Not because you hide what upsets you, but because you can freely share what upsets you, and that opens up more space for sharing more things that your partner does to fill your tank.

I hope you stop keeping score... except in ways that make you both feel like winners.

And I hope that one day—maybe years from now—your children look back and realize that what you built together wasn't perfect, but it was intentional. It was generous. It was real.

That's what a Relationship Millionaire really is.

So, my wish for you isn't just that your love lasts.

It's that it grows richer.

That it deepens.

That it teaches.

That it heals.

And that when life gets chaotic—and it will—you'll remember that the best investment you'll ever make isn't in a stock or a business...

It's in the heart of the person lying next to you every night.

You're not just building a relationship bank to get you through hard times. You are building security to know that you are better together.

With love,
Dina

Examples really help to see how this works, but I don't want you to use it as a blueprint. I want you to do what feels right to you when it comes to awarding and taking away money. Use the following example to see harmony-disharmony-repair patterns and then apply it to your own lives.

Maya & Daniel: Three Days Toward Becoming Relationship Millionaires

DAY 1 – MONDAY

HARMONY

The clock reads 6:12 a.m. Maya goes downstairs, her hair still messy from sleep, heart heavy from last night's 2 a.m. toddler wake-up. She could have slept another 20 minutes. But she would rather do something nice for her partner. She brews his favorite coffee, adds milk, two sugars, and cinnamon, and leaves it steaming on his desk beside a sticky note: "You've got this today. Love, M."

+$1,000 (Maya – Unprompted emotional labor + small act of love)

Daniel walks in a few minutes later, rubbing sleep from his eyes. He stops. Smiles. He goes to find Maya and says, "You seriously make me feel like the luckiest man alive." He kisses the top of her head.

+$750 (Daniel – Verbal affirmation + physical affection)

Later, Daniel handles school drop-off like a pro. Backpacks packed, lunches grabbed, the toddler's sippy cup remembered. Maya watches him drive off and exhales with a full heart.

+$800 (Daniel – Anticipating needs without being asked)

She texts: "You crushed it this morning."

He replies: "We're a team."

+$500 (Maya – Expressing appreciation)

+$500 (Daniel – Reinforcing unity)

That night, they belly-laugh watching their toddler's dance moves. It's one of those moments where everything—time, bills, worries—fades away.

+$600 (Maya – Family joy)

DISHARMONY

Dinner is chaotic. Maya is finishing emails, a pot is boiling over, and Daniel is scrolling on his phone while sitting at the table. The weight of the day lands hard.

"Can you please help instead of zoning out?" Maya barks.

Her tone cuts deep, and Daniel's body stiffens instantly.

–$500 (Maya – Harsh tone, lack of grace in communication)

"Sure," he snaps back. "Because I haven't done anything all day, right?"

–$600 (Daniel – Sarcasm + emotional shutdown)

He walks away without helping. The distance between them expands.

REPAIR

After the kids are asleep, Maya walks into the living room and sits beside him. She doesn't touch him. She just says, "I didn't mean to come at you like that. I was drowning."

+$1,000 (Maya – Vulnerability + ownership)

Daniel puts his arm around her. "I get it. I was tired and took it personally. Let's go pick something from the mistake jar to do." They write three new things and pick out one Maya put in a few weeks ago. It says finger paint on each other's faces with ketchup. Daniel laughs at how ridiculous the suggestion is, easing the previous tension. They get ketchup and paint on each other's faces. Hey, this is pretty fun. They share a long, intimate kiss in between painting each other's faces with ketchup.

+$1,000 (Daniel – Humor + forgiveness + reconnection)

They lean in and breathe together, no need to fix it all—just a willingness to feel together again.

Net Total Day 1: $5,050

Note to the readers: If we polled 100 couples, there would be a lot of different reactions to finger painting ketchup on each other's faces. One couple might think it's hilarious, one partner might be upset that they could get acne from the ketchup, one partner might say now they feel stuck with cleaning up the mess of ketchup all over the kitchen, and they don't like the feeling of ketchup all over their face. One partner might think it's a waste of ketchup, while another partner might say they feel all gross and sticky and don't have time for a shower now before work.

Sometimes, attempted repair rituals make things worse, and that happens. You can, in an honest communication, continue to drain the love tank until you find the thing that brings back filling up the love tank. One of the worst things you can do is "fake it" by pretending that your partner filled up your love tank to spare their feelings. Don't lie about your body and your love tank. It's not good for the relationship long-term. It might make your partner feel a false sense of security that they repaired and you are back into harmony, but false harmony actually deteriorates a relationship over time and builds resentment.

DAY 2 – TUESDAY
DISHARMONY

They wake up still a little raw. The ketchup face painting was fun, but afterward Maya did all the dishes alone while Daniel finished a work project. Maya makes eggs while thinking that she alone cleaned the kitchen last night. She doesn't want to deduct money because the ketchup face painting was so fun; she wants to build on the positive energy. Daniel sips his coffee. Maya starts sharing about a work presentation she's nervous about:

"I don't know if I'm even qualified to pitch this," she says.

Daniel barely looks up from his phone. "You'll figure it out."

–$400 (Daniel – Emotional dismissal)

Maya feels it. The air leaves her lungs. She wanted support—not a solution. She doesn't argue. She just goes quiet.

That afternoon, Daniel asks her to pick up milk. She forgets.

When he opens the fridge and sees it missing, he sighs, "Guess dry cereal it is again."

–$350 (Daniel – Passive-aggressive comment)

She shrugs, but her chest tightens. *I can't do anything right*, she thinks.

She walks into the bathroom and cries quietly while brushing her teeth.

–$250 (Maya – Emotional self-abandonment + silence)

REPAIR

That night, Maya takes out her journal. She writes: "I wanted you to believe in me today. Instead, I felt brushed off and invisible."

She walks into the bedroom, sits down, and reads it to him.

Daniel puts his phone down, looks her in the eye. "I'm sorry, M. I was distracted, and that's not okay. You deserve someone who's with you."

+$1,250 (Maya – Sharing emotional truth + not bottling it)

+$1,250 (Daniel – Accountability + eye contact + validation)

He takes her hand. "You'll crush that pitch. But if you don't—I'll be proud of you for trying."

+$500 (Daniel – Repair through reassurance)

They fall asleep with their legs intertwined.

Net Total Day 2: $2,000

DAY 3 – WEDNESDAY
HARMONY

Daniel wakes up early and leaves Maya a protein bar, her vitamin, and a little Post-it that says: "You're magic."

She sees it and instantly smiles.

+$1,000 (Daniel – Forethought + emotional intimacy)

She walks into his office, leans against the doorframe, and says, "You're sweet."

+$500 (Maya – Receiving + verbal affection)

They spend five minutes laughing over their toddler's new obsession with talking to their smart speaker. "Alexa, play fart sounds!"

They're both laughing.

+$600 (Daniel – laughing)

DISHARMONY

Later, Daniel is getting dressed for an important Zoom call. He searches the laundry basket. His shirt isn't there.

"Maya," he calls sharply. "I asked you to throw this in the wash yesterday!"

–$500 (Daniel – Accusatory tone)

Maya freezes. Her cheeks burn with shame.

How could I forget again? I'm such a mess. He needed me. I failed him.

She says nothing. She just turns and walks away.

–$600 (Maya – Emotional shutdown + shame spiral)

REPAIR

Daniel feels bad about treating his wife poorly over a shirt. He was frustrated that it wasn't clean, but there was no reason to scream at her.

He texts her. "I came in hot. It wasn't about the shirt—it was about feeling out of control. I'm sorry. I didn't mean to make you feel small."

He clicks "send."

+$1,250 (Daniel – Digital repair + naming his emotion)

Maya sees his text, sits quietly for a while, then writes a note on a heart-shaped sticky and leaves it on his bathroom mirror:

"Your shirt is clean, pressed, and on the bed. So proud of you. So proud of us."

+$1,000 (Maya – Thoughtful repair + pride in their progress)

They end the night wrapped around each other. No words needed.

Net Total Day 3: $3,250

THREE-DAY GRAND TOTAL: $10,300

This couple is not perfect, and not always graceful. But they are aware and have some level of accountability. This challenge is about letting your partner into your inner world. The things that really sting, they might not realize. The things that they are beating themselves up over, letting you down, might not have actually drained you very much. The point of all this is that the repair mechanisms you are trying to evaluate internally now have a numerical value. You can be confident that if your partner is approaching the challenge with honesty, when you have numerically repaired what drained your partner's love tank, you can feel confident you are back to a state of harmony. If you quickly go from harmony back to disharmony, there is more repair work to be done. If you have a major issue and you put a band-aid on it, there might be a short feeling of repair, but your partner, if they are honest, will let you know their love tank is still drained. That's okay and should be a welcome form of communication. The most important thing to remember is that hidden feelings lead to quiet resentment and slow decay of a relationship. Even though a state of disharmony can be uncomfortable, it is so much better for your relationship in the long run to address the disharmony and figure out a way to repair it. It might not be the first repair attempt that works. However, if you are determined to repair and get back to a state of harmony, don't stop trying repair techniques until your partner feels their love tank is filled.

I wish you the best of luck in your journey. I hope your real-life examples can help open a line of communication that really and truly enriches your bond to feel the security that you have a strong, unshakable relationship!

About the Author

DK Moench is an author passionate about helping couples strengthen their connection through better communication and understanding. As a homeschool mom and lifelong learner, she has spent years exploring what makes relationships thrive when two people see the world — and express love — in completely different ways.

Inspired by her own marriage to her high school sweetheart, Tim, DK wrote *Relationship Millionaires* to bridge the gap between partners who don't always "speak the same language" emotionally or mentally. She believes that being different from your partner isn't a flaw — it's an opportunity to grow, connect, and deepen your love in ways that feel genuine and lasting.

Through her writing, DK empowers couples to embrace challenges as pathways to closeness rather than conflict. Her mission is simple yet powerful: to help partners feel more confident not just in their relationship, but in how they feel about each other every single day. She lives in Cherry Hill, New Jersey, with Tim and their four sons, where she continues to learn, teach, and encourage the beauty of growing together.

I wanted my relationship to be the best it could be. That desire—the simple but powerful decision to stop settling and start growing—is what inspired Relationship Millionaires.

Somewhere along the way, I realized that many couples fall into the same patterns over and over again. We often attract someone whose personality mirrors or challenges our own—and the cycle begins. But when we start to see those patterns clearly, we also start to see our power to change them.

This book is for every couple who wants to build something extraordinary together. It's for the ones who know their love has potential but feel stuck behind walls of silence, misunderstanding, or fear. Because let's face it—what's going wrong in a most relationships today isn't lack of love; it's lack of communication.

If not now, when? If your love is truly the most valuable asset in your life, then it's time to start treating it that way. You can work hard, make money, and chase success—but without a deep, connected relationship, even the greatest achievements can feel empty.

I'm not a therapist or a relationship coach—I'm someone who married my high school sweetheart and learned firsthand how easy it is to struggle even when love is real. Through that journey, I became obsessed with understanding what truly makes relationships work, and how couples can transform everyday frustration into lasting connection.

The purpose of this book is simple: to help you better know where your partner is day to day and how your interaction is impacting them—and to help you build the kind of communication that turns love into secure love. When you master connection, and you are confident you are on the same page as your partner you become a relationship millionaire.

Throughout these pages, you'll be challenged to look deeper, communicate better, and show up for love in a way you never have before. You'll see what's been holding you back and learn practical ways to break through it—together.

By the end, I want you to do more than just finish this book. I want you to take the challenge, put these ideas into practice, and then pass it along to a friend who needs it too. Because being a relationship millionaire means more than having wealth—it means building a love so strong, it inspires others to do the same.

Follow along and share your journey on Instagram at @relationship.millionaires

Let's make your relationship your greatest asset.

🐟 Charitable Dedication

To my dear friend Cheryl Piggot, founder of The Stars Foundation,

Whatever your current financial status may be, one of the most powerful actions you can take on your journey to becoming a Relationship Millionaire is to give—whether it's your time, your resources, or your heart.

One of my favorite organizations in the world is The Stars Foundation. Founded by Cheryl Piggot, a woman with one of the kindest hearts I've ever met, this foundation has brought hope to vulnerable children around the globe, many of whom are orphans. Cheryl's mission goes beyond charity—it is a legacy of love.

If you're in a position to give this year, I'd be honored if you visited their site: www.thestarsfoundation.net

If you make a donation, please let me know at dinamoench@gmail.com. I would love to personally thank you with a message from my heart to yours.

To give some perspective:

- If you make $25,000 a year, you're in the top 10% of global income earners.
- At $50,000, you're in the top 1% globally.

As you read this book and do the inner work of transforming your relationship into your greatest asset, I invite you to also open your heart to those who could truly use a helping hand. Giving isn't just about money—it's about energy, intention, and remembering the children in the world who are navigating life without parents.

Every single dollar matters. Whether you give $1 or $1,000,000, it all adds up—and it all makes a difference.

> *"We make a living by what we get, but we make a life by what we give."* — **Winston Churchill**

Relationship Millionaires don't just build wealth—they build meaning. One of the greatest acts of love is to lift another human being.

With all my heart,
Dina Moench

www.ingramcontent.com/pod-product-compliance
Lightning Source LLC
Chambersburg PA
CBHW061703120626
46550CB00003B/1068